CHARACTER INSIGHTS FOR A REGENERATIVE FUTURE

5 Leadership Superpowers
to drive Growth, Innovation
and the Future of Work

ENDORSEMENTS

"I have long admired Paul Steenkamp, both as a profoundly decent human being and as one of the smartest thinkers on innovation and leadership around. How fabulous that through his book others now get to benefit from his expertise and experience too! "Character Insights for a Regenerative Future" makes for powerful and deeply personal reading. It is an indispensable guide for all of us who have wondered how to build quality relationships between people of good character and so doing, create much needed islands of sanity and possibility in our world."

Niven Postma, MD of Niven Postma Inc., HBR and Inc. Africa Contributor, Author and Lecturer on Office Politics, Strategy and Culture Consultant

"Paul Steenkamp has been crucial in rallying us around new ways of working and thinking."

Johannes Wedenig, Convenor, UNICEF ESARO

"The work Paul and his team do help test the power of innovation to transform us into a more fit-for-purpose humanity."

Zinzi Mgolodela, Director: Corporate Affairs, Woolworths South Africa

"Paul is an awarding winning innovation leader. He has an uncanny ability to anticipate how the business world is changing in response to technological advances. But even more impressive, Paul has the ability to lead and galvanise innovation teams to respond positively to disruption. He understands that breakthrough innovation cannot be done using traditional management tools, and he is able to help large corporations adapt cutting edge tools for developing creative new products. As an innovation leader, Paul is absolutely world-class. It was an honour work with him and I would do it again in a heartbeat."

Dr. Tendayi Viki, Author of Pirates in The Navy *and Associate Partner at Strategyzer*

"What I value second most as a client, is that Paul is a thought leader on innovation. He has paid his school fees implementing innovation programs in large corporations and so is able to design and co-create interventions with you because he has tried and failed; learned, unlearned and relearned. As a client, this means you can learn from the mistakes he has already made, in an effort to make new mistakes of your own!

But what I truly value most about Paul and his team, is the intention of their work. At the heart of it, it's about making a difference, being part of the solution. There is nothing better for me, from a South African consultant."

Lauren Benjamin, People and Organisation
Business Lead at Sanlam Investments

"Paul has been a contributor on leadership development and design thinking courses I have been involved with since 2018. Paul's work is an extension of who he is and I thoroughly enjoy working with him. He brings much experience, warmth, wisdom and mind-bending insights to the table. He has a lasting impact on those who design and execute new innovations - especially in large, mature corporates. His war stories - told with authenticity and ownership of his own successes and failures - ensure that his session ratings are consistently excellent, and a very hard act to follow. "

Dr Nadine Mayers, Executive Education Convenor & Facilitator
Thinking Partner & Founder @ Xtra-Ordinary

"Respect."

Helena Conradie CFA, former CEO, Satrix

"Paul Steenkamp has been instrumental in unlocking fundamentally different thinking to solve very complex business challenges using the design thinking methodology and approach."

Jonathan Loder, Head of HR: ROG and Organisational
Effectiveness, Woolworths South Africa

"Lots has been written about innovation leadership but what Paul has managed to capture in this book is priceless. Drawn from years of hands-on experience and insights of leading and navigating teams who operate deep within the innovation engine rooms of legacy organisations he has distilled critical reflections, readings and learnings that every leader interested in growth and innovation must know.

Fundamentally Paul identifies that successful corporate innovation is based on "quality relationships between people of good character" and in *Character Insights for a Regenerative Future* he unapologetically captures critical character traits that leadership must have if they hope to achieve effective innovation outcomes."

Richard Perez, Founding Director of the
Hasso Plattner d-school at the University of Cape Town

First published in 2022.

ISBN: 978-1-86922-948-1
eISBN: 978-1-86922-949-8

Published by KR Publishing
Tel: (011) 706-6009
E-mail: orders@knowres.co.za
Website: www.kr.co.za

Typesetting, layout and design: Cia Joubert, cia@knowres.co.za
Cover design: Marlene De Lorme, marlene@knowres.co.za
Editing & proofreading: Jennifer Renton, jenniferrenton@live.co.za
Project management: Cia Joubert, cia@knowres.co.za

CHARACTER INSIGHTS FOR A REGENERATIVE FUTURE

5 Leadership Superpowers
to drive Growth, Innovation
and the Future of Work

Paul Steenkamp

with **Tanya Meeson**

FOR JANÉNE

"One of the most beautiful gifts in the world is the gift of encouragement. When someone encourages you, that person helps you over a threshold you might otherwise never have crossed on your own." – Lyrics from the song *Praise You* by Fatboy Slim:

> *We've come a long, long way together*
> *Through the hard times and the good*
> *I have to celebrate you, baby*
> *I have to praise you like I should*

ACKNOWLEDGEMENTS

It takes a village to raise a book. The author is grateful to his wife and daughter, Janéne and Olivia, for juggling to help find book-life balance; to his friend and writing partner, Tanya Meeson, without whom this book would not exist; to his Granny Peggy for instilling a love of writing; to his Mom for instilling a love of storytelling; to his inspiring friend Niven Postma for leading the way and introducing him to the intrepid publisher Wilhelm Crous and the team at Knowledge Resources; to the purpose-driven Katlego Maphai (CEO & Co-Founder of Yoco Technologies) for sharing insights from his journey; to clients and former employers for the mentorship and learning opportunities; to his friends, Kevin Liebenberg (CEO - The Actuate Group), Graham Fehrsen (Founder and CEO - NOVO), Bianca Bosch (New Business Innovation and Ventures, CIB) and Sarah Rice (Chief People Officer - Skynamo), for providing feedback on the manuscript; and lastly, to the pioneering Fred Keil (KRW co-founder and author of *Return on Character*), Angela Duckworth, Rosa Lee, Egbert Chang and Dave Levin (Character Lab Co-Founders) for blazing the trail of scientific insights that help the kid in all of us thrive.

TABLE OF CONTENTS

ABOUT THE AUTHORS

Paul Steenkamp is an advisor, author and investor. He is grateful to serve makers, rebels, and dreamers doing good differently.

In 2016, he founded Jack Frost, an effective problem solving consultancy for executives and their teams.

A former corporate innovator and innovation leader, Paul was part of the executive committee of Standard Bank's Personal & Business Banking and headed up the award-winning FNB Innovators program when the bank won the Most Innovative Bank in the World title.

For six years, Paul has served South Africa's parliament as a National Advisory Council on Innovation committee member.

His qualifications include an Executive MBA from Henley Business School and Honours in Industrial Psychology from Rhodes University.

He is an alumnus of the SingularityU South Africa Executive Programme, the THNK School of Creative Leadership in Amsterdam and the online Saïd Business School, University of Oxford. Paul is also an accredited Think Wrong Instigator and a proud Solve Next global partner.

You'll find Paul hanging around in Cape Town, being walked by his dogs, or packing and unpacking the dishwasher.

Tanya Meeson is an author, columnist and journalist with a special interest in relationships, psychology, transformational leadership and health. Her work has appeared across a wide range of media including *Mail&Guardian, JSE, African Decisions, Marie Claire, Woman&Home, Cosmopolitan, 24.com* and *HEAIDS*.

PREFACE

One of the things that led me to writing this book about the corporate innovation space was getting fired from it.

At the time, this is not something I would've happily admitted to or been able to laugh about. I'd initially been hired by the firm, a major legacy corporate, to head up their innovation drive and my ego was deeply invested in the role. So deeply, that when it all came to a quiet but lawyered-up end, it took me a long time to process how my actions and beliefs had contributed to the collapse of my relationship with the company.

When I walked out of the exit talks, I was initially relieved, but this was eventually overrun by an emotional tsunami of not only rejection, but also guilt and shame.

I'd been part of a great team that had taken initiative and helped to deliver some great innovations and impact. We'd believed we could help improve the organisation's innovation capabilities and we did. But I'd let my ego get in the way. I hadn't fully realised and appreciated the opportunity to make a positive impact on the lives of millions of people in businesses across the continent. I'd let down those who had helped me while I was there; I'd stopped telling the truth as an Executive. I'd let my emotions control my short-term decision making. I'd failed to connect with enough colleagues, customers and communities, and had not been curious enough about their most pressing problems. I was a premature evacuator. My capacity for intellectual humility had been zero. My grit score was pathetic.

It was not the last time I'd make those mistakes though.

After years of working on both sides of the table, as a corporate leader and corporate advisor, I've had my share of stops and starts, hits and misses. But whichever way my work has looked, life has led me – sometimes gently, most times kicking and screaming – to the gift of these transformative events, and these, I believe, have ultimately taught me what the true driver of great innovation is.

I am now more convinced than ever that it starts with leadership character and ends with trust and great relationships. My aim with this book is to convince you of that. By drawing on the work being done by researchers and thought leaders across multiple disciplines, I hope to make a case for this. If nothing else, I hope it will start a conversation about what it means to be a better leader broadly, and to be a better leader for effective corporate innovation specifically.

And there has never been a better time for this.

As our societal and economic structures shift in an increasingly VUCA world, it's more important than ever for businesses to modernise their ways of thinking and ways of working to match and adapt to these changes. Leadership, too, must adapt, managing the dual demands of preparing for the future while optimising for today, tapping into their people's creative energy and collective wisdom to maximise the great advantages their purpose-driven problem-solvers can add to the business.

Getting agile and getting innovative is no longer a 'nice to have' for leaders and legacy organisations; they're imperative mindset and process changes for business sustainability.

If you're here, it means you've seen this too. It means we're in the same boat together, pointing in the same direction, looking for new ways of doing things.

Maybe you're a leader in your organisation; maybe you've been given a mandate to run an innovation programme or initiate new ways of working. Maybe you're just an interested boundary-pusher or you've started to feel a sense of urgency around doing things differently. Wherever you are in your organisation, this is leadership work. Going against the tide and doing things differently requires all the traits required of a modern leader: grit, intellectual humility, curiosity and the grace to learn new things – and unlearn the old.

Leaders rich in these qualities are already here. These are people driven by their intrinsic motivation to make a positive impact on the world. They're the ones who know they're lucky to have corporate jobs with access to a big balance sheet, a big brand, lots of data, legislative licence and millions of customers. And they're leveraging these assets to serve others and the planet. They're the ones who know that the upside of corporate innovation is impact at scale. I know they're there because I have the privilege of working with a few of them. It's how I've been able to verify for myself that people of great character are essential to successful corporate innovation.

I must add here, that although this book is premised on supporting innovation in the corporate space, this theory on culture and leadership character is not just about the corporate arena – it applies to anyone in a leadership position in any group context. I've just kicked off from here because it's my background, but I believe this message about leaders of good character has stretch across all organisations, not least of which is our national leadership. This isn't to say that I've gotten this whole 'person of great character' thing right myself. I've gotten it very, very wrong. I've been a jerk. I've messed up. I've played the politics badly and chased my own tail one too many times. How I form and build relationships in the innovation space is something I've had to work on. My character traits have had to enjoy the shit sandwich of uncomfortable realisations and adjustments and continues to do so.

But I believe that sharing war stories can help us learn and do better next time. Organisations, just like people, are desperately imperfect, and my work is to help leaders and their teams make them a little less imperfect. My experience is by no means exhaustive; I bow to the work done by people much smarter and more experienced than me. I don't have all the answers, but I've got some good ideas about which character traits work and which ones don't. And if that can help you save some precious resources (most specifically people's non-renewable time at work) by not making all the mistakes I've made, then that's a good thing.

PART 1

THE GROUNDWORK

A few years ago, Pieter Swiegers, who was then the Corporate Investment Bank's Head of Digital at Standard Bank, asked me what the secret to successful sustainable corporate innovation was. I found myself hesitant. It was a big question and I wanted to give him a meaty and impressive answer. So I did. I gave him the most erudite best-practice consultant-speak answer I had. It sounded great. It was perfect. It was the kind of answer an expert puts up on a presentation slide and pauses, while conference delegates photograph it and post it to LinkedIn. It sounded good, but it didn't feel authentic and I hated it.

I hated it because it didn't feel true for me. Sure, I had a lot of experience in the machinations of corporate innovation and how it might work. But the secret sauce that pulled it all together? Well, I hadn't quite nailed it in a way that felt authentic for myself.

Later that week, I sat around the table with a group of innovation specialists from different organisations in a wide array of industries. We were all there as part of the Creative Leadership Collective, a peer-to-peer advisory network I'd started in the hopes of providing support for local corporate innovation leaders, and we were unpacking the difficulty of forward movement in big companies. This kind of conversation was just all too familiar in these meets. Over the course of a few months, we'd shared our experiences in the process work of innovation: methodologies, systems, theories... But every time we'd get through what we were doing and how we were doing it, we'd inevitably end up at one point: what an uphill battle it was to actually do it.

On that particular day, I was sitting around the table listening to the same issues come up – lack of leadership buy-in, team breakdowns, Exco distrust thanks to many false starts, impatience for the innovation pay-off and so on – when I started seeing the underlying problem emerge. That's when I realised, I hadn't been blindsided by the enormity of the answer to Sweiger's question but by the simplicity of it. Because the short Mark Twain answer to his question wasn't yet another process or another, newer, glitzier business model that needs to be brought in from Silicon Valley and plugged in for our local reality. No. The secret to successful corporate innovation was much simpler than that. It was simply 'good relationships'. More specifically, perhaps, 'quality relationships between people of good character'.

We were all sitting around this table bitching because we were having relationship problems with our colleagues and leadership teams.

This was a big a-ha moment for me.

A few years before, I'd been inspired to take a mini-sabbatical to do some field research in the States. My mission was to visit modern schools dedicated to developing the capacities of young people to become innovators. At the time, I was heading up FNB Innovators (a grassroots employee innovation program) and had watched the TED Talk 'Do Schools Kill Creativity?' by the late, great Sir Ken Robinson. It became one of the most-watched TED Talks of all time with (as I write this) more than 72 million views. Sir Ken had sparked a hypothesis within me: Could companies learn from the principles, practices and processes leveraged by 'Creative Schools' to help unleash their innovative employees? Long story for another day, but this got me onto KIPP, the Knowledge is Power Program, founded by Dave Levin and Mike Feinberg in 1994.

Like many other charter schools, KIPP was designed to help break the cycle of poverty by offering a viable path to high school graduation and college for their low-income students. However, by 2009, KIPP found that six years after finishing high school, only about one in five of their New York City alumni had earned a college degree. This was major realisation. For most learners, the assumption that a high school diploma was enough to break the cycle of poverty proved to be incorrect. At that point, KIPP began shifting its focus to developing kids who were more than just great 'test-takers'. In 2013, Levin co-founded The Character Lab, a non-profit organisation on a mission to 'advance the science and practice of character development' with a focus on kids. I can only assume that this move influenced KIPP to do things differently and do different things. By

2016, the four-year college completion rate of KIPP's alumni had risen to 45%. Coincidence? I think not. Overwhelming scientific evidence now demonstrates the link between character strengths and achievement (including physical health, and social and emotional well-being).

As much as I wanted to explore this field of early childhood development, nurturing creativity in kids wasn't where life was leading me. Where it kept leading me, for my sins, was to boardrooms and office blocks, to C-suiters hungry for change and future-forward HR execs eager to find ways to prep their people for new ways of working. It kept leading me to innovation practices and radical problem-solving. It kept bringing me back to the question of how to be a better innovation leader and how to coach the leaders I work with in this space. If developing character was such a defining element for children, why not adults? Why not leaders in innovation?

I was already very familiar with the work done by thought leaders and researchers looking into various aspects of leadership character and how it affects business in general. The work done by Fred Kiel is a particular stand-out. And being in the innovation space, I was familiar with the many books that have been written about innovation strategy, structures, practices and processes, and those trying to define what they believed to be the ideal start-up culture underpinning the ideal environment for innovation.

But there always seemed to be a disconnect between those two conversations – 'leadership character as it affects business' and 'innovation' – in the corporate arena.

The only place 'leadership', 'culture' and 'innovation' seemed to intersect was within the start-up conversation. Even then, I usually felt like character was too often confused with 'personality', and that 'culture' was either too casually referred to without much definition or just taken for granted to mean the general 'vibe of it all'. We're told to learn from the high growth start-up founders and how they set the tone for the business, but there never seems to be a specific look at how exactly they're setting that tone. What is it about their specific character traits that influences this? The only place I was used to seeing 'culture' or 'character' unpacked fully was in research deep dives that never see the light of layperson day.

That day of the CLC meet-up where I had my first realisation about relationships and corporate innovation surfaced a big question for me: If my secret to successful corporate innovation was 'quality relationships between people of good character', then how was that to come about? What was the interplay between 'leadership character', 'culture' and 'innovation' within the corporate space? How did the two connect?

Some answers and connections started emerging: I believe the strength of a leader's quality character traits extends to the company's capacity to respond with agility and speed to the market. I believe that good character traits support good relationships and build trust – all of which are necessary to support this kind of agility.

But there was one more addition to this realisation: that the idea of 'successful' innovation must be broadened to 'effective and sustainable' innovation. More on that later.

Character Insights for a Regenerative Future is a tentative first offering of which leadership character traits matter to effective innovation outcomes. The choice of the five specific traits was extrapolated from my experience with innovation in the corporate space, but also from the relevant work being done by disparate groups of researchers and thought leaders in various fields of study.

Reality bites

Before we get to the juicy stuff, I think it's worth painting a bit of a picture of where we are currently in the corporate innovation space, locally speaking. And I can sum it quickly for you if you're time poor and want to move on to the next chapter. Here it is: It's messed up and it's getting worse.

That's the short of it. The long-ish of it is this:

The *Science Technology and Innovation Indicators Report* tracks the health of South Africa's innovation prowess relative to the rest of the world. It's produced by NACI, the National Advisory Council on Innovation, and it's their flagship product.

As a member of this council, I've become increasingly alarmed by their findings. For the last five years, we've kept slipping further and further back as a nation. There's a lot of criticism of the report. Some say there's too much information, that it's too big and therefore meaningless. Everyone gets distracted about how the report is formatted and what it does and doesn't have.

But in focusing on this, the point is missed: we're falling behind at an alarming rate.

At a country level, we can attribute this to the lag of a failing education system and a shrinking economy. At an organisational level, and generally speaking, I believe the problem sits with the conservative nature of those execs at the feeding trough who guzzle up their short-term bonuses regardless of the health of the company and the people it employs. They don't really care about whether the company is going to be successful in 10 years' time or whether the country is going to be successful for the collective. What they care about is keeping the status quo as immovable and safe as possible, while investing their personal wealth offshore until they're ready to take their sign-off bonuses and head elsewhere.

There are other problems of course, but this general theme of short-termism in both macro- and micro-structures in South Africa affects not just effective and successful innovation in terms of existing products and markets, but the ability of legacy organisations to utilise the best of innovative thinking and radical problem-solving to adapt their systems for the future. Because both require leadership capacity to rethink ways of working and to let go of the reins a bit. And, in the midst of our current situation, letting go and trying something new must seem like too great a risk. Rather better to keep things quiet; keep them stable.

But in staying quiet and keeping the status quo steady, we slip further and further behind on the global stage.

Look, I know there is nothing that poops a party quite like focusing on the negative. I see this happen in my client workshops when we're doing a deep dive into empathy work, either looking at the pains of the customer or the organisation. It often brings the energy down and bums people out. This is especially true as we move from identifying symptoms to underlying causes, when everyone's getting real about the company's systemic flaws and the cultural issues in it. Framing the real challenge that emerges from this can get uncomfortable and sometimes borderline antagonistic. But as any problem-solver worth their salt knows, problems are where the heart of the opportunity lies. And if I'm going to unpack my theory about what lies at the heart of culture, we should be clear about what this culture currently looks like in the one place we really want to affect change: the legacy organisation.

Poking the giant

Our legacy organisations are large, complex beasts, most of which have large, complex, problematic histories with an internal culture that lends itself most comfortably to the institutionalised hierarchies of the past. Trying to affect organisation-wide change overnight is impossible.

Very often, even when the executive leadership puts up a show of being as faux start-up as they can – they can say it's all about being multi-disciplinary and egalitarian – at the end of the day, innovation culture inevitably finds itself rammed against the hard paunch of corporate culture leadership: a bloated cadre of line managers who've been eating the shit sandwich for 25 years and now that they're finally the boss, choose to be radicalised custodians of the status quo. If you've been around long enough working in the corporate innovation space, you'll probably have found yourself at the dead end that is this paunch. And it can look like any number of situations.

Maybe the person leading the executive team left and all attempts to do things differently fell apart after that, or you couldn't get buy-in from the people at the top. Maybe the international consultants and the great, hugely expensive system they brought in fell apart on practical, local application. Maybe the top brass couldn't see the money rolling in quickly enough and so cut you off, or infighting and politics strangled your team before it could do anything worthwhile. Maybe inertia set in and interest to change or innovate around your system or product fizzled away into the daily humdrum of business as usual. Change is difficult after all, so why bother? Or, my personal favourite, the 'close the gap' team arriving with a licence to immediately reassign every innovation resource to Sales or sayonara so that the short-term Exec bonuses get paid.

Maybe, even worse than all of that, you've done all the things you were asked to do and you did them well: your value proposition was sound, your business model was sound, you spoke to your customers (internal or external) and you were certain you were meeting a real need, but your team fell apart because the politics around it damn near killed you and all you were left with was waste and disillusionment.

Great stuff. Welcome to the corporate innovation space.

So why even bother?

I actually started thinking of calling those CLC peer-to-peer advisory meet-ups 'Innovators Anonymous', because it often felt like a bunch of puzzle junkies who believe in healthier organisations and the power of effective innovation just getting together to commiserate and pat each other on the back (hell, no one else is going to it) while murmurs of "Fuck. It's so hard. It's so fucked up!", filled the air. And yet, no one was jumping ship to go mortgage their homes on a start-up idea they had while brushing their teeth.

Why not?

Because the corporate innovator, the intrapreneur, is an entirely unique animal. The intrapreneur is the person who intuitively knows the benefits of their employers' competitive moat. In a country like ours where the economy is unstable and the margins thin, the tiny start-up dinghy heading out into rocky seas are really at the mercy of the bad economic currents and the unpleasant weather conditions of the ruling party. Their founders are more likely to get smashed against the rocks of a wildly insufficient Venture Capital sector than ride it out for that nine-year overnight start-up success payday – if it ever comes.

Locally, at least, the big corporate ship is where we have the opportunity to disrupt from the inside out. Established companies simply don't struggle with the same problems that entrepreneurs do. Legacy organisations have the money, brand, customers, data, resources, human capital, a regulatory licence and the reach to make real changes that are significant – not just to their bottom line, but to the society they're part of. I've seen this happen. I've been part of radical problem-solving initiatives with major South African companies that have seen their staff paid more, created jobs and their ways of working streamlined to the benefit of their frontline staff and customers. Most enticingly to natural intrapreneurs, these organisations are also full of inefficiencies and ineffectiveness; a veritable hotbed of juicy optimisation problems for any puzzle junkie. Throw them the hook 'because it's the way it's always been done' and they'll be the first off the mark to find ways of building and evolving, doing things differently, doing them better.

The intrapreneur isn't necessarily in a leadership position. They might even be hiding in the unsexy office rooms of Accounts or Legal. Not every radical problem solver is starting their own company; not every radical problem solver *wants* to start their own company. Despite the many cultural blocks and traditional hierarchies to contend with, they know that there is value in being an innovator in a large organisation.

Sure, start-ups can show us the way forward; we can learn from them, their agility, their flexibility. They're disruptors and they keep us on our toes. But the time of vaunting start-ups as the only place where real change can happen is coming to an end. Looking to them to change the system is imbalanced and, in South Africa, implausible, especially when promising start-ups often get prematurely and aggressively acquired by incumbents. Moreover, start-ups are not where the problem lies, and as such are not where the opportunity is.

This isn't to say that it's easy for the person tasked with changing that big ship's direction or prepping it for another 20 years out at sea. It's stressful and risky. It's very much unchartered territory. The nature of what we're doing isn't about sailing into a calm Mediterranean Sea. We're launching into vast unknown oceans and most of us are having to convince the ship's crew and captain that they have no other option. We're still inventing the future. For many, it's scary stuff. There's a lot of pain. Like I said, 'Innovators Anonymous' seemed to be a viable alternative name for the CLC Meetups.

But that's what I love about it: when the variety dial is turned up to 11 and my adrenaline kind of kicks. I'll take the scariness and the stress of what we're talking about any day, because I've seen the profound difference that doing things differently can have on people's experience at work, the corporate culture, the company's clients, and its bottom line. Even the positive impact it can make on society. The prospect of helping to bring positive change at scale through corporate innovation is my path.

Hopefully, your experience won't need to be quite so choppy, but it is likely to be. When you push against the behemoth, it pushes back. That's how you know you're making progress.

Collectively, getting to a company culture that embraces innovative thinking, that lives and breathes it, is going to take time. There are no easy solutions, no shortcuts. It's simply one foot in front of the other. Hopefully, *Character Insights for a Regenerative Future* will go some way in shedding some light on how you tread.

Working on the ecosystem, not just in it

I believe that there are four major misconceptions when it comes to the idea of 'innovation', and they all connect with the same fundamental issue: we're working on the wrong problem.

1. We often think of it only as a product

Getting agile and getting innovative is no longer a 'nice to have' for legacy organisations. It is not optional. Not every broken and unequal organisation realises this yet, but that's the truth of it. However, we need to update our concept of what innovation is.

The usual response to 'getting innovative', especially in terms of big organisations, goes something like this: A company needs to boost its bottom line and it needs a shot of new energy, something to show at the next analyst meeting, so it hires a fancy growth incubator or a big, external think tank or consultancy to come up with a new product or service. Maybe it goes so far as to build its own internal innovation capability, sporting all the bells and whistles of innovation theatre – setting aside a small, curious group of B-team mavericks and loose ends to brainstorm new products in a room full of FatSaks and ping pong tables.

Although innovating products and services for customers is an important piece of what we do, it's not the only type of innovation that can be utilised in and for organisations. I'm a big believer in McKinsey's Three Horizons Framework, which outlines how businesses should invest in three different types of innovation.

a) **Core**: Optimising existing infrastructure, products and services for current customers.

b) **Adjacent**: Converting existing infrastructure to develop new markets that expand the customer base.

c) **Transformational**: Designing an entirely new business model from scratch; doing things the company has never done before in markets that are new to the company or new to the world.

The framework initially included time horizons, but these have subsequently been challenged by the rate at which we can innovate using modern technology. Nevertheless, the three types remain valid. When we meet to talk about innovating within a large company, we need to agree which type of innovation we're ultimately after and, ideally, agree to invest in all three.

Regardless of how you channel your focus, learning how to think, problem-solve, respond and collaborate like an innovator is where the great and urgent need lies for large organisations. Already, some pioneering legacy companies are adopting innovation practices and philosophies to update their business models and ways of working to deliver innovations across the full spectrum – from core to adjacent to transformational. They're doing so with the aim of becoming more agile and responsive to market fluctuations and competitors, thereby better serving both their external and internal customer base.

This is really where innovation practice can take us. This is how innovative thinking can make our businesses stronger and better prepare us for the future.

When companies, especially big, legacy organisations, limit themselves to the view that innovation is simply about making newer 'things' or delivering newer services for existing customers, they limit their potential to adapt and retain relevancy for their current and future market base and employees.

2. We rely too heavily on the cult of the visionary leader

There is a still a myth, thanks to the power of the Steve Jobs image in the world, of the visionary leader as the beating heart of continuous innovation in an organisation. We're familiar with the stereotype and there are certainly enough of these in other start-ups to perpetuate the story. As for the legacy organisations, well this might be a slick firebrand CEO or the senior leader intrapreneur who has the ear of the Board or powers that be to make sweeping product and image changes.

While the visionary leader can fire up the motivation for innovative thinking and new ways of working in the organisation, the fire they bring very often also fizzles out when they leave. I've seen it happen more than once.

The power of an organisation's innovation drive cannot rest with one person. Creating this key person dependency poses huge problems. When they move on, the system around them risks collapsing, because the energy and charge that that one powerful, committed and passionate leader brought to the collective is removed. This leadership element is necessary but not sufficient because it is not sustainable, nor is it maximising the collective's talent.

3. We confuse innovation tools with the innovation itself

Which brings me to the third problematic perception: that innovation methodologies and practices are considered the innovation itself; that when a company or leader adopts an innovation practice, they consider their innovation boxes immediately ticked.

Anyone who's been in the corporate innovation space in any capacity for 10 years, a year or even a month, will be up to their eyeballs in podcasts and books around the role of leadership, strategy and organisational structure. They'll be drowning with all the cool concepts and Silicon Valley literature of innovation strategy management and practice offerings: Open Innovation, Lean Start-up, linkages, Lean, Agile and human-centred design, among many others... all of which work and all of which are moving parts in the methodology of innovation practice. In my own work, I use Open Innovation, Lean and Design Thinking as a matter of course. They're indispensable for creating structure and maximising the practice of innovation.

But it's all too easy to stop here; to fall in love with these pretty, shiny, well-packaged methodologies and processes that come our way. We make the mistake of becoming obsessed with them, focusing solely on them as if they are the very source of the innovation itself. We get wrapped up in their story: combining processes, taking elements out, tweaking them and so on. And we inevitably start believing that each of these is the magic spell that will instantly turn our organisation into an innovation powerhouse.

In and of themselves, however, these methodologies and practices are not sufficient to drive sustainable innovation outputs – whether those outputs are products or new ways of working – because they don't solve the underlying issues that support or hinder the implementation or execution of the innovation they're there to serve.

Rather, these methodologies and processes should be thought of as the tools that leaders use to drive innovation *inside* a supportive innovation ecosystem, rather than as the ecosystem itself. Think of them as the seed, not the soil that will ultimately support its growth.

4.   We still define growth as increasing profit

Our obsession with short-termist, 'profit over principle' economic growth has seriously damaged our habitat. Up until now, the innovations of our time that have been considered the most successful have been driven by profitability rather than human need and with little regard for our limited resources. The underlying culture of legacy organisations has been one of gouging, value extraction and short-term benefit. I believe this needs to change if business is going to survive.

Inspired by the Effective Altruism Movement, I believe that we must adopt the concept of effective innovation, defined as, "innovation that uses our resources (which are now precious and scarce) to improve the world now and for future generations". If we hope to have any semblance of a stable social, economic and environmental context in which to operate our businesses, this must be our new gold standard when thinking of 'innovation'.

What is the ecosystem?

Whether we're looking at innovation as core optimisation, product development or systems change, it doesn't happen in a vacuum. It succeeds – or fails, as is often the case – depending on the ecosystem it finds itself in.

Innovative products can't live without the infrastructure to support them: trains can't exist in the world without tracks, medical drones can't exist without government legislation and ports, Tesla can't exist without its own unique set-up to support its unique creations.

Likewise, no new processes or methodologies to create agility and innovation robustness will succeed in an organisational structure that doesn't want or support this. Throw that methodology seed on cement and you're not going to get much rooting; throw it in rich, loamy soil and you're more likely to reap some veggies later.

This ecosystem, then, is the context in which the innovation work is being done and can be seen in both a macro and micro context.

The macro context for me is well-defined by IDIA, the International Development Innovation Alliance, which outlines the innovation ecosystem quite exhaustively as "enabling policies and regulations, accessibility of finance, informed human capital, supportive markets, energy, transport and communication infrastructure, a culture of supportive innovation and entrepreneurship, and networking assets, which together support productive relationships between different actors and other parts of the ecosystem".

In a far less wordy fashion: the micro context is the organisation you find yourself in and all its associated moving parts. While the two contexts deeply influence each other and there is an argument to be made for country leaders also getting a thorough brushing down on their character traits to determine their efficacy and how this might benefit business and a forward-thinking economy, it's this micro context that I'll be focusing on in the book.

The innovation ecosystem is an organisation's structural capacity and appetite for innovative thinking. In other words, the internal systems, processes and cultural dispositions that – depending on their health – either drive and enable the implementation of sustainable innovation outputs, hinder it, or, as is so often the case, just downright kill it. The value of a supportive ecosystem is greater than the visionary leader. It surpasses the importance of the methodologies that are introduced to it. In my experience, if we're going to implement any strategy successfully, the ecosystem is where the real work lies.

So how do we know what it looks like? I believe the key word in seeing and understanding the health of your particular organisation's ecosystem is 'implementation'. It's in the implementation process, and how smoothly or painfully it unfolds, that the strengths and weaknesses of the organisation's innovation ecosystem are laid bare. Implementation is where lip-service is shown up for its bollocks and where all the cultural skeletons rattle out of the closet: you can't talk your way through experimentation and you can't push change through a system that's bulldozing back.

Implementation is where performance management contracted by line managers, risk audits, top-down hierarchies, the culture of perfection and institutionalised fear of failure – all those stalwarts of risk-averse big business – reveal themselves. Current thinking tells us that if you can solve the problems that your customers and constituents have faster than your competitors, you'll be a more successful business. But you can't move with agility if your ecosystem is sludge.

Implementation: The ecosystem's health status indicator

Innovators like to say that talk is cheap and processes open source; say whatever you want to say, take whatever you need, because implementation is everything and that's the really hard part about innovation. And yet, a lot of implementation is itself approached like a plug-and-play process: use this methodology and follow these one-two-three steps and you'll get sign off on a job well done.

Experience, however, has shown us otherwise. Those of us who've been in the game long enough know that implementation is rarely, if ever, this easy. Despite this, I don't know how much recognition there is that successful implementation reflects the uniqueness of the organisation – that it isn't a copy and paste job and that it can never be this.

If your innovation ecosystem isn't set up to support your progress, you're going to burn a lot of fuel designing an innovation orphan that goes off into a corner to die because it's an unfamiliar, clumsy fledgling, unwanted by the time-poor custodians of the operating business tasked with operationalising it but who never asked for it in the first place.

This is why the implementation process has become an area of deep interest for me. It's the door to the big questions about the ecosystem: What are the organisational dimensions helping or hindering innovation? Why does it look this way? Why isn't this working? Who needs to move, shift, get onboard or jump ship for this to work? How can we best achieve this here? What needs to change for real forward movement to happen? What does this say about the team? What does this say about leadership? What does this say about the company's capacity to integrate innovation principles into its structure?

These aren't traditionally the questions associated with implementation. More common questions might be 'Does the customer like this?', 'What have we learned (about the product) from this or that experiment?', 'Do we need to pivot, persist or kill'... that sort of thing. And although this is a fundamental part of implementation, it's a very superficial awareness if it's the only takeaway you have from the process.

We need to move beyond the implementation conversation as an end in itself, and ask ourselves rather what it says about the ecosystem it's operating inside and how it might improve.

Working on the right problem: innovate the system

I'll repeat: The power of innovation doesn't lie in sexy strategies, going digital, adopting Agile or Lean or Design Thinking, or even the promise of emerging technologies. It isn't owned by a visionary leader. It doesn't lie in popping out another product. I believe that we've come to focus on products and these methodologies and technologies almost exclusively without creating and optimising the soil for the good innovators and innovations to grow.

The power of innovation lies in building this structural strength, this internal ecosystem, so that *whatever* problem you throw at the organisation, it's able to turn that missile into an opportunity or bat it away. Ultimately, it becomes capable of adapting to whatever volatility, uncertainty, complexity and ambiguity the world throws at it.

Modern organisations, including large, complex ones, are good at solving their own problems. They've innovated their organisation and so have the ecosystem – the internal systems, processes and cultural dispositions – to do so. They've done this because they know that it doesn't matter how good their products, services or business model are; if their ecosystem isn't supportive of change, there's going to be no way to implement any of their solutions over the long term. Most importantly, there's going to be no way to respond to the radical shifts in the macro environment.

To get to this point of strength, where we can improve innovation outcomes and modernise workplaces, we need to be prepared to dig deeper and get our hands dirty. We need to do the 'think slow' work. We need to move beyond doing work only at a process level and look at the context supporting it. In effect, we must stop merely working *in* the ecosystem and start working *on* it.

I believe that we begin this work by stopping. We stop simply treating or ignoring the symptoms of innovation ill-health that crop up during implementation and instead use them as markers for where the ecosystem can be strengthened. If we're getting push-back from leadership, we need to investigate what must be innovated in the structure of influence. If we're getting tangled up in company processes and procedures, we must innovate to streamline. If Legal, Risk and Finance keep getting the way, we must innovate to bring them on board and build trust.

Effective corporate innovation involves improving the health of the ecosystem. Just like human bodies need to get healthy from the inside – eat well, get some rest, play some team sports – organisations need to get healthy from the inside by building their problem-solving muscles and structural agility, learning how to collaborate and increase transparency, and introducing interventions that support its immunity to life's rough and tumble.

So, where do we start?

It's my belief that we start with the ecosystem's most fundamental element – culture – and then go a step even further than that.

Character might crack the culture code

Over the past few years, I've come to realise that my clients aren't really buying my help to design strategy or solutions anymore. They come with a juicy strategic problem they're trying to solve, and although that problem might initially present as a restructuring issue or a process or product problem, their situation invariably always boils down to people putting their needs ahead of their customers' and other related faults in the organisation's culture.

We understand an organisation's culture to be those group norms, values, beliefs and assumptions it practices. It's what defines how the organisation's processes are formed, who it hires, how decisions are made and how the company evolves – or *if* it evolves. Because no matter what problem you want to solve, what strategy or restructuring you need to do, nothing can move it forward if solutions or experiments to solve are derailed by legacy mindsets: overly cautious risk management, distrust, lack of accountability, favouritism or political stonewalling.

Collectively, we've come to know these issues as 'a culture problem'; that ill-defined phenomenon that often seems to creep out of nowhere or feel as fundamental to the business as its brand, values or logo. It might express itself as boredom and stagnation or the fear of failure, anxiety and distrust. It looks like a lack of communication, a power hierarchy, crippling KPIs linked to short-term rewards, too many processes and policies, a limpet-like attachment to the status quo, a shark tank executive...

'A culture problem' is damaging over the long term. It can't riff with the disruptors and it isn't agile enough to consider doing something different. It's what made Kodak leadership decide they didn't 'do' digital and Nokia cling to its hardware user experience instead of shifting to expand its data and software offering. It's why Xerox didn't exploit its PC lead and Blackberry dropped out of smartphones. These companies are routinely paraded as examples of how legacy companies failed to create an innovation culture, in other words, how amped the organisation's innovation ecosystem is to support agility and problem-solving. In these cases, clearly not very.

But these and other laggard legacy companies have one more thing in common beyond this generalised 'culture problem'; their lack of innovative thinking was as a direct result of leadership and the decisions those at the top made. And there's nothing vague about that.

In *Innovator's Dilemma*, Clayton Christensen shows that innovation problems are often inextricably linked with a resource allocation problem. A company's innovation resources are typically distributed based on the views of its execs and hotshots. If they have a dim view of an innovation, it doesn't get assigned the resources and human capital. If the executive team in charge of the golden keys isn't willing to open the doors to external collaborators, pave the way for agility, or listen to their people and customers, there's no way they're going to be able to build a modern organisation fuelled by innovative thinking. This is especially apparent if, when it comes to disruptive innovations, there isn't enough data (or any data) to prove them and their HIPPO tendencies wrong. (HIPPO is an acronym for 'the highest paid person's opinion' and refers to the cultural tendency to defer to the person who gets paid the most, regardless of whether they're right or not.)

So, what was it about these leaders that made them unable to see beyond their own limitations? What was it specifically about them that stalled progress? What was it about their character that set them up for failure to innovate?

We can ask the same of any leader in any organisation today.

If we want to create a supportive innovation ecosystem, I believe we must first look to answer these questions. Because beyond culture are the people who come together to create it – people driven and informed by their own personal character traits, traits that include or exclude, build or break, seek to catapult into future possibilities off a launchpad of deep trust or cling to present success in a stormy sea of unsustainable inequity.

Character: A hypothesis

It is my hypothesis, then, that leadership character, not organisational values, is the most basic building block of organisational culture. If you really want to assess the culture of your company, assess the character of the people creating it. If you want to change the culture of your organisation, you've got to change – swap out, bring in, develop and strengthen – the character of the people creating that culture.

I know, given the vast swathes of research and complicated diagrams dissecting organisational culture, that this is a bold statement to make. Cracking the culture code – how to change it, improve it, understand it – has seemed like an elusive Holy Grail for decades. It's been the organisational psychology of alchemy: discovering how to change your leaden culture back to the gold that gifted your organisation the momentum that has gotten it this far.

But I believe this is it. If you want to strengthen your 'innovation culture', if you want to build an innovation ecosystem, go to its most basic building block at the deepest level of its foundation: leadership character.

Before we go further, however, it's probably best for some clarity around what I mean by 'character'.

'Character' is very basically defined as the mental and moral qualities distinctive to an individual. Someone displaying good character follows a moral imperative that underwrites their actions.

Here's a scenario. You're at the shopping centre and you've got your bags of groceries piled up in the trolley. You push the trolley out to your car and unload its heaving contents into the boot. Now your trolley is empty. What do you do with it when nobody is watching? Do you push it to the side behind the car next to yours and leave it there, or do you push it back to a collection point, out of everyone's way?

During the Covid-19 pandemic, an anonymous Reddit post presented this scenario as a litmus test for whether people would be able to self-govern and be generally good humans. It went viral. The idea was simple: Would an individual do the right thing without being legally forced to? In other words, would you push the trolley back simply because that's the right and considerate thing to do? Or would you leave it where is comfortable for you and make it someone else's problem?

The question was raised in terms of self-governance around mask wearing and social distancing and so on, but I think it speaks directly to character. Because one measure of your character is how you treat your environment and other people – especially those who are not close to you or those you perceive to be in a lower power position than yourself – when there's no apparent gain for you to do so.

Character is not personality

The last few decades of organisational psychology have seen a significant dedication to the cult of employee assessments based on the personality. The same can be said for companies trying to find their way to better staffing outcomes.

Away from the researchers' desks and into the HR hubs of the organisations themselves, you'll find this single-minded obsession with personality. You'll be familiar with, I'm sure, the array of personality assessments for anyone and everyone across the organogram: the Myers-Briggs Type Indicator, DiSC Assessment, the Predictive Index, the Five-Factor Model of Personality... and on and on. There's especially a lot of work being done now in the innovation community around profiling different personality types associated with innovation. It's usually something along the lines of The Creator, The Cowboy, The Doer, The Helper, The Scout and so on.

The basic idea of personality tests is that if you can tweak the mix of your team's personalities to just the right proportions, you'll get better cohesion, collaboration and team spirit. And if you can secure the extroverted leaders with just the right levels of pep and vim to rally those teams, nothing will be out of your reach.

But personality is surface. Where character refers to the moral attributes or qualities of a person, personality refers to the collection of cognitive abilities, behaviours, beliefs, ideologies and attitudes that that person presents to the world.

Personality cannot be defined as either right or wrong; you have a sense of humour or you don't, you like to engage with people or you don't. Character is objective. Personality tends to change when a person is put under pressure, character tends to be reinforced under pressure. Personality is an immediate expression observed in physical conduct with the external. Character is the moral and ethical driving force of the internal.

Think of character as the inner self and personality as the interactive mask we employ with the outside world. Personality is who we are and what we do when everyone is watching; character is who we are and what we do when no one is watching. There's a brilliant quote by Elma G. Leterman, author and 'master insurance salesman' of the mid-20th century: "Personality can open doors but only character can keep them open."

Unfortunately, whenever anyone starts speaking about character, they invariably default to speaking about personality. Even though what constitutes 'good' and 'bad' character has long been studied and debated in one form or another as part of the human sciences, research into what good or bad character means for business, leadership and success is an emerging science. There's certainly no definitive list of character traits that define good leadership or bad. Each study, some of which I mention in the next chapter, surfaces its own collections of traits as more or less valuable, either in the context of leadership or success.

My hope is that *Character Insights for a Regenerative Future* will go some way to adding to this conversation. Part 2 of this book will surface the specific character traits that I believe support innovation in a corporate context, the traits that will serve any future-forward leader or leader in training. These strengths are hardly extensive – they're simply those that I have found, in my experience, to be the most valuable. Each chapter is its own character trait, and within that chapter I will illustrate through experience and studies why each is valuable.

Character trumps talent, skills and expertise

Talent, skills and experience are often applied as heavily weighted criteria for recruitment or promotion. This is starting to feel like it needs an update. Skills and experience are derived by games we're taught to play in the system – from school to university to our first experiences of the workplace. If you can memorise the text books, you know how to work the 1-2-3 steps of the system; if you have the networks or if you're simply conversant in the language of industry, you can sail through an entire career, as a radicalised custodian of the status quo, maintaining it *über alles*, and cashing in on the short-term financial incentives while failing to innovate – even in the face of dire social, economic and environmental upheaval.

In 2016, when I started the process of validating an alt MBA in partnership with Richard Perez and the d-school (The Hasso Plattner School of Design Thinking at the University of Cape Town), what we learned from many big corporate employers was that a high ratio of the people with lots of skills and experience, those who presented really astonishing CVs, can be especially problematic when it comes to the traits required of modern leaders. Generally speaking, they've often got the skills and experiences because they've been brought up within a very privileged context with all the entitlement that engenders. In South Africa, specifically, they earn disproportionately more than their contemporaries in other emerging markets, and often attach their sense of self-worth to their inflated salary.

But talent, skills and experience alone do not redefine sectors. It's the people who have a strong intrinsic motivation to push through the barriers to change to make a difference. These are the people who display the character strengths of grit; who are purpose-driven; who, in the long run, redefine their sectors and outperform their peers exponentially. Those characteristics are their defining qualities, not their skills or experience.

It reminds me of the widely quoted Ellen Winner line from her paper, *The Origins and Ends of Giftedness*, which she published as a psychologist in 2000. "Only a fraction of gifted children eventually become revolutionary adult creators," she writes. "Those who do so must make a painful transition from a child prodigy (a child who learns rapidly and effortlessly in an established domain) to an adult creator (a person who disrupts and ultimately remakes a domain)."

When you're trying to build or rekindle a culture of innovation, talent, skills and experience are qualifiers, not differentiators. At the time of writing, the top 10 companies by market cap between 2018–2019 were new – none of them were top 10 years ago – and the average age of those companies is less than 20 years. In other words, people who are running the biggest companies in the world might not be as skilled and experienced in the traditional sense as people running the companies that are maybe 11 to 20 in the top biggest companies, but they're running more successful companies.

So I'm suspicious of talent, skills and experience as the only motivating factors behind hires and promotions, especially at an Exec level. Sure, they are necessary, but they are insufficient as standalone inputs. If I look at how organisations are aiming to generate value and remain competitive, I'm most likely to place my bets with the group of purpose-driven, gritty collaborators looking to move the company into the future – a group of individuals who are ready to learn and unlearn, fast and often. This option is better than an Exco team with all the talent, skill and experience, but who are constrained by a know-it-all sense of entitlement and penchant for short-term bonuses linked to maintaining the status quo.

If talent, skills and experience are not the stand-alone clincher to stay relevant by leading effective innovation, if they're not what makes a future-fit, modern leader, I have to wonder, what would happen if we started recruiting with good character traits as the baseline? After all, what good is skill and experience if your expensive hire is an asshole guaranteed to carpet-bomb your organisation with drama that rips your team apart and erodes your customer focus?

The culture DNA of your business is set first by the character traits of the founders and then the management team

Although it's my hypothesis that a company's culture is the manifestation of the character traits of its leaders, I believe there's a disproportionate impact on culture made by the founders and those sitting on Exco.

I believe most companies start with a similar DNA, which can broadly be described as other-centred: a group of people, typically led by a charismatic leader, see a problem in the world and get together because they're excited about solving it; they have an intrinsic motivation to solve it in ways that create value for decades and generations to come. The group is typically other-centred in that they have empathy for the people experiencing a problem and they want to help solve that problem. The next step is obvious: once they solve the problem, they start figuring out how to make money out of solving the problem. Most successful organisations start like this.

But then the conundrum: they become victims of their own success. They do such an excellent job of solving the problem they're passionate about that they risk running out of cash trying to service exponentially growing demand. So they do a deal with the devil – the VC funding circuit, shareholders – trading their discretionary decision rights and long-term vision for the much-needed, massive cash injection to scale. They slot into traditional modes of doing business to fulfil the requirements of their macro contexts: the processes, the procedures, the bureaucracy. They then either hand over to a board and shareholders, or control solidifies with the charismatic leader.

Enter the Horseman of the Corporate Innovation Apocalypse – pay that rewards professional managers for short-term success.

In most cases, the new majority shareholders are impatient investors chasing quarterly returns. They put a Board in place to protect their investment by overseeing the implementation of politics that boost profits for them. The Board is incentivised to deliver 'growth' via a cadre of professional managers – executives and managers motivated by perverse salaries, bonuses and benefits.

The character traits of these short-term-minded shareholders, institutional investors, executives and professional managers ultimately become solidified in the company's ways of working that are reflected in the new hires they bring on board. And we are all prone to hiring mini-mes. Employment bias is the unconscious bias in hiring practices where the people who get hired look like the people who wrote the code for hiring them. New employees will track the character traits and personality of the executive team and so the circle continues – the culture of the start-up-turned-big-company is slowly, silently set.

There's traditionally an almost 'viral' effect in this culture dispersal. When founders of good character form the culture of the company, they will inform and hire accordingly; the executives and managers will emulate their leadership style and the workforce will respond in kind. The opposite is also often true when these founders are displaced as the majority shareholders.

Bad character is a rot that spreads

In 2018, Rob Arthur, a US journalist covering criminal justice and politics, published his work 'Bad cops spread their misconduct like a disease'. The piece was an investigation into the policing networks of Chicago and was based on data collected by the Invisible Institute of more than 30,000 police officers and almost 23,000 complaints against them between 2000 and 2018. By augmenting and processing these data, the institute was able to create a massive social network of police interactions, tracking specifically those that flagged bad actors. What they discovered is that like attracts like: cops with a bad rep tend to gravitate towards each other. But it goes further than that, writes Arthur. "The data shows that they also may be teaching their colleagues bad habits."

Using the Invisible Institute's data, he chose a large set of cops with low complaint rates before 2008 and then split those into two segments: 863 who'd been listed on a complaint with officers at the centre of the network, and 12,815 who hadn't.

"The officers who had been exposed to the contagious, misconduct-prone cops at the centre of complaint networks went on to show complaint rates nine times higher over the next ten years than those who hadn't... The data is rich with examples of young officers whose trajectories bent toward misconduct after exposure to bad influences."

I believe the same can be seen in organisations. Think of it as a cancerous cell: a small character flaw in the executive team that, left unchecked, spreads and grows. It's a copy of a healthy cell that's just slightly corrupted and then, due to employment bias or the corruptibility of bad character, copies again and again, so that the corruption gets exponentially bigger, eventually infecting the entire organism – damaging its health and threatening its longevity. This corruptibility doesn't have to be cruel or even necessarily evil, it could just be a risk-averse or fear-based trait.

I don't mean that organisations need to have founders or executives of perfect character. No-one is perfect, especially me, so I realise that's not possible. No one scores high across all character strength dimensions. We each have a unique combination of high- and low-scoring dimensions, but depending on the weakness and the position of power the leader holds, it can have a detrimental impact on your organisation's capacity to innovate effectively. The longer the organisation runs under a flawed cadre of professional managers, the more the bad character traits spread until eventually you look back and you can't reconcile the organisation's culture to the character strengths of the original founder.

Good character creates high-trust relationships

You'll find two words repeating often throughout the book: trust and relationships. Part of my hypothesis is that being mindful of character and developing character strengths through practice forges high-trust, high-quality workplace relationships. These relationships provide the safe space within which innovation thrives for the long haul.

Good character (leads to) → good relationships = trust = great innovation outcomes

I believe this is the real secret to effective and sustainable corporate innovation.

Great Place to Work, the global authority on workplace culture, regularly surveys employees of companies that have signed up for the service to track worker satisfaction and experience. They've surveyed millions of employees from organisations around the world over three decades and have found a "clear and direct relationship between employee engagement and financial performance". Most importantly, they've revealed that low engagement is due to a lack of trust.

In the lead up to their 2016 Great Place to Work Conference, Anil Saxena wrote: "Woven throughout the companies that make up the Fortune 100 Best Companies to Work For list is a foundation of trust that permeates everything those companies do. In a High-Trust culture, employees don't have to focus their time on trying to decipher corporate speak or worry about if their jobs are secure. Instead, they can spend their time creating exceptional products, powerful customer experiences and lasting relationships at work."

The high-trust relationship pays off for everyone, says Saxena. Leaders know that they're supported in doing what they need to do to navigate the complex and changeable business environment, and employees have the peace of mind to keep performing no matter how bumpy the ride.

And yet, the value of high-trust, high-quality workplace relationships is a conversation that's been woefully under-represented in the innovation space over the last few years. The closest corporates can bring themselves to acknowledge trust as a valuable social capital resource is usually when they're trying to manage messy trust events that affect their customers' view of their products or service and threaten the business' bottom line. Just think of the value of customer trust in the Fourth Industrial Revolution when data breaches occur and personal information is flouted.

But the trust I'm talking about here is about building structural integrity into the bones of the company, into that ecosystem. In other words, building trust within your workforce, between you and your employees, between management and their people, and within teams.

Solid relationships between people of good character will build the ecosystem of trust necessary to innovate consistently. No attempts at innovation or modernising an organisation will succeed in the long term without this. Nothing else matters in the innovation lifecycle – not how good your innovation strategy is, how good your innovation practices or processes are, how good your innovation management is, or how digital your technological infrastructure is.

This might be difficult to accept in the corporate space. When it comes to the interpersonal nuances of the workplace, the corporate straitjacket has restricted the words 'trust', 'relationships' and 'good character' to the limits of a soft skills issue; matters that are best left to HR execs, Chief People Officers and ethics committees.

And yet, without trust there can be no effective collaboration. Without trust there can be no calculated risk-taking – not on the company's side or the employees'. Exco needs to trust the inherently risky unknown of the new horizon enough to invest resources and see the implementation process through each incremental result. Employees need to trust leadership so that they don't feel ridiculed for 'crazy ideas' or be branded troublemakers for being radical problem solvers and poking holes in the business model, strategy of theory.

Without trust, Exco and that Horseman of the Corporate Innovation Apocalypse will kill an innovation before it's implemented. Without trust, employees attracted to engaging in innovation projects or looking to be intrapreneurs might fear the consequences of failure: lost promotional opportunities, dismissal, a dead-end career path. The innovation process requires huge amounts of trust and the flow of trustworthy, non-combative communication between gatekeepers and those doing the work.

Think of it this way...

Imagine you're putting together your team to survive the Zombiepocalypse and you're going to be heading out into unchartered territory, where the journey is uncertain and the destination mostly guessed at. Oh, and you're going to be dealing with attacks from the lumpen braindead that want to kill you around every corner. Are you going to choose your team based purely on their skillsets alone, or are you also going to consider how much you trust someone or how well you understand each other? Is it worth having the guy who can hunt if he's just going to keep the catch to himself, or worse, cannibalise your team when your resources are low?

When the going gets tough, you're going to need to trust the person next you – the one that's supposedly got your back. Hell, you don't even need to imagine the end of the world. Right or wrong, you know that in big organisations especially, without a good relationship with the person that matters, nothing you do or want to do is likely to see the light of day.

Quality relationships matter. Trust matters. But what builds good relationships is the character of the particular people in the relationship. So character matters. When you're choosing your team for the Zombiepocalypse, you'll be looking at skillsets, sure, but you'll also want to consider those aspects of their character that contribute to good relationships, such as their other-centredness, empathy, courage, grit, loyalty and so on.

And as for that person in your workplace environment who can make or break your plans? How does that ego and power-wielding bode for the company as a whole?

Forging high-trust relationships depends on good character

Trust isn't a plug-and-play feature. It's not as simple as buying everyone pizza on a Friday or introducing Casual Wednesdays. This might be difficult to accept for leaders who have never had to question or self-reflect on what it means to actively build trust in relationships. There is a deep connection between the capacity to build trust and character.

Ken Dovey is the Director of the MBITM programme within the Faculty of Engineering and IT at the University of Technology Sydney. He's done considerable work in the field of innovation and his paper, *The Role of Trust in Innovation*, goes a long way to unpack these trust drivers. It's a worthwhile read for anyone interested in doing a deep dive into this topic, but I was particularly interested in the steps Dovey believes leaders can to take to build trust in the corporation and what this says about their character strengths.

In these four 'building blocks', Dovey uses South African President Nelson Mandela's actions at the time of the 1994 democratic elections to illustrate his findings.

*Building block 1:
Identify stakeholders
and reach consensus
on the core (mission,
vision and values)*

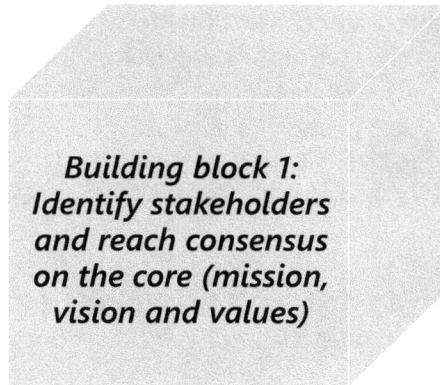

"Mandela's first strategy was to establish the Council for a Democratic South Africa in which every political party – irrespective of its ideology and size – was given a seat at the table to establish the basis of a new constitution (or core) for the country."

The idea, Dovey points out, was to establish a "win/win orientation to the strategic task of building trust". Through this strategy, he says, Mandela recognised those who had a stake in the future of the country and, via the creation of a negotiated order, ensured that their voices were heard. In business, this translates to identifying stakeholder groups, recognising their value in the firm and convening them around a shared goal.

"The innovative capabilities of organisations often depend solely on the intrapreneurs within their midst", says Dovey. They're the ones who have the grit and tenacity to push through even while risking their own future within the company. This kind of courage "usually stems from the deep trust that they have in the mission of the organisation – an endeavour that resonates directly with their personal, or existential, value proposition".

Building block 2:
Respect the other

There was nothing soppy or politically correct about the presidents's concept of respect, says Dovey. Mandela's respect for the inherent value of all human life meant that he treated all equally, regardless of status or race. "To build trust in this way", writes Dovey, "necessitates the abandoning of notions of superiority, of ego and hubris and relating to others on an equal footing". This speaks directly to the non-hierarchical structure of teams in the problem-solving space.

Building block 3:
Honour commitments

Dovey recalls a function Mandela attended early in his presidency. "Upon Mandela's entry the band struck up the new national anthem for South Africa but left out sections from the old anthem that had been included as part of the reconciliation agreement. Although such an omission was popular with the majority of those attending the function, Mandela ordered the band to replay the anthem and, this time, to include all sections of it."

Dovey makes the point that Mandela was in this way reminding his supporters that everyone had agreed to a set of commitments that had to honoured. This generated huge trust in him because even though he now had political power, Mandela was a man of his word.

"Too often business leaders fail to honour the rules in their everyday behaviours", says Dovey. "Expedience tends to supplant principle when convenient, while the mission, vision and values espoused in public can fail to be enacted in practice."

This is particularly important for leaders to bear in mind: what's good for your people, has to be good for you.

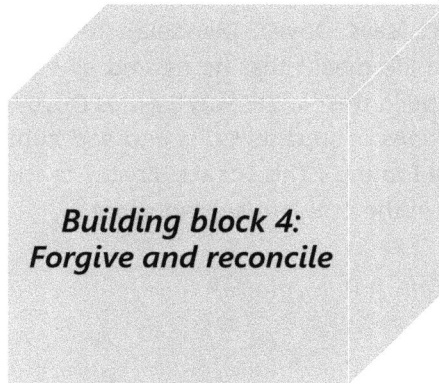

Building block 4:
Forgive and reconcile

The Truth and Reconciliation Commission, led by another iconic, courageous, moral crusader, Desmond Tutu, was a master stroke for healing the emotional wounds that apartheid had inflicted on South Africa's people, says Dovey. "Mandela explained his rationale succinctly: without sincere confession there can be no forgiveness; without forgiveness there can be no reconciliation; without reconciliation there can be no peace."

Cases of fraud and legal twists aside, there is a lot leaders can do to facilitate new relationships and to recognise, and overcome, the structural bases, such as hierarchy and functional silos, of much mistrust in organisations, says Dovey.

He highlights establishing a culture of 'straight talk' and honesty; of accountability and personal responsibility for mistakes; of principle and the courage to honour it; and of commitment to a cause greater than oneself.

"Such behaviours," he says, "would be a refreshing change from the half-truths, finger-pointing, scapegoating and defensive self-justification that we often witness through the media with respect to political and corporate leaders and which erodes public trust in governments and stakeholder trust in a business".

Already we're seeing the value of TRC-type interventions in the corporate space. South African businesses in particular are providing the platform for employees and leadership to hold courageous conversations around diversity, inclusion and equity in the context of the inequality, unemployment and violence that continues to plague so many of our communities.

There's a reason Nelson Mandela has become a global icon of upstanding character, and Dovey's use of this to explain trust in organisations is on point. After all, what can get bigger than leading a national organisation?

As a leader, having the capacity to build trust in your business comes down to one core aspect: your character and the characters of the other company leaders involved. It's not that you have to be a Mandela, but to build the sort of trust environment that fosters continuous innovation, you need to be a person of good character. As a leader, to be committed to making a meaningful contribution to the world and having passion and perseverance for long-term goals is both purpose-driven and gritty. To respect and connect with those around you as equals and problem solvers, rather than subordinates and drones, reveals a capacity for social intelligence and intellectual humility.

Believing you can improve your abilities while recognising your knowledge's limitations displays a growth mindset and intellectual humility. To be able to build a value set that you yourself honour while drawing like-minded people together points to a level of integrity and capacity for collaboration. These character strengths are part of a modern leader's arsenal.

Looking forward to the 21st century

Good character strengths – of leadership, of the people in your team – is at the base of it all. From this we can build trust and from there solid relationships. This is the foundation supporting, influencing and driving your strategy, your practices and your processes, and then only from there, your tech and product.

Without getting the fundamentals right first, you're not going to be able to build the problem-solving muscles and adaptability to respond to your customers and constituents faster than your competitors can, consistently and continuously. And if you can't do that, there's no way your business is going to be prepped for the long game. All you're likely to see will be incremental wins consisting of doing the wrong thing righter or wins that will eventually be cut short, whether you're looking at innovation across any of the three horizons or laying the groundwork for new ways of working in your organisation.

To prepare for business in the 21st century, you must have the people with character strengths fit for the 21st century.

The case for character

Doing something without any apparent gain for yourself is a concept in direct opposition to leadership born out of the 1800s Industrial Revolution, honed to a razor-sharp edge in 1900s capitalism, and surviving like a desperate parasite into the start of the 21st century. Considering that unethical business practices and leaders have made our world economy what it is today, for better and worse, it's tempting to dismiss relationships and character as part of the basket of soft skills that gets set aside as an optional extra in management and business studies. Until recently, these sorts of 'soft skills' just haven't been considered fundamental to a company's paramount purpose: a good business model and growing that bottom line. But these 'soft skills' and this idea of 'good character' matters to both.

Being a leader of high character affects your bottom line

In 2015, researcher, adviser and author Fred Kiel published his ground-breaking book, *Return on Character*. His previous book *Moral Intelligence* had gone so far as to anecdotally suggest that high character leaders get better sustained long-term business results than low character leaders.

But although this concept had seemed obvious to him, the negative reaction to it was intense. In his talk, 'Psychopaths in the C-suite', Kiel recalls: "The push back was strong. [We got told:] 'Don't tell me that; you're a psychologist and all that soft stuff is nice to have but isn't really essential as long as you stay legal. What really creates value is the business model and this [character stuff] is just the frosting on the cake'."

Kiel took this feedback to heart and accepted the challenge to find the supporting data with his team at KRW International, a Minneapolis-based leadership consultancy. They wanted hard business metrics and chose to focus on two: the return on assets and the level of workforce engagement.

To get this information, they set up a national research study aimed at understanding and researching the connection between character and business results, enrolling a hundred CEOs from Fortune 100 and Fortune 500 companies, privately held firms and non-profits. They asked random samples of employees (in total they got about 8,000 employee observations) to rate how well their CEO demonstrated four principles, namely integrity, compassion, responsibility and forgiveness, and then created a single character score from these results.

What they found confirmed their instincts that there was a significant return on great leadership character. Those businesses whose CEOs had been rated highly on these character strengths by their employees enjoyed an average return on assets of 5.3% over a two-year period. This was nearly three times as much as businesses whose CEOs who garnered low character ratings. Their ROA averaged only 1.93%.

The difference was even more startling when it came to leaders who scored the highest and lowest on character. While the highest character leaders, what Kiel calls "virtuoso CEOs", contributed an average of 8.39% return on assets, the lowest character leaders, who he jokingly refers to as "the almost psychopaths", actually made a -0.57% loss for investors.

When they looked at levels of workforce engagement, says Kiel, they tracked exactly the same.

"When a CEO or a leader of any kind demonstrates integrity it tends to generate trust in the workforce. When they demonstrate responsibility it tends to be inspiring to the workforce. When a leader or CEO demonstrates forgiveness, that's what generates innovation in a workforce and when they show compassion, that's what drives workforce engagement and talent retention."

What comprises his four principles then – integrity, compassion, responsibility and forgiveness – is really an outline in two parts of what makes a *mensch*. Kiel divides these four principles into two groups: the head and the heart.

The 'head' principles are integrity and responsibility. In his definition, integrity competencies include acting consistently with principles, values and beliefs; walking the talk; telling the truth; standing up for what is right; and keeping promises. Responsibility means taking responsibility for your personal choices, admitting mistakes and failures, embracing responsibility for serving others and to committing to "leave the world a better place".

Then there's the two 'heart' principles of forgiveness and compassion. Forgiveness is the ability to let go of your and other people's mistakes, while compassion drives workforce engagement and talent retention.

Ultimately, says Kiel, high character leaders create high energy, positive work environments where people love to work, which leads to greater talent retention and better output, which eventually translates to lower labour turnover and better performance on that bottom line. Low character leaders, on the other hand, create environments that shut people's creativity and motivation down, inspiring only the will to leave the company.

Down the rabbit hole with the dirty hands

Kiel and his research partners didn't thumb-suck those four principles – they were the result of the team's synthesis of previous work done by Donald Brown in the late 20th century. An anthropologist and author noted for his work in defining the behaviours and characteristics recognised and displayed in all human societies, Brown coined the concept of the 'Universal Person' (UP), outlining this UP's characteristics in his book, *Human Universals*. Drawing on that list, Kiel and his team identified those four moral principles – integrity, responsibility, forgiveness and compassion – as universal traits and took their cue from that.

It was as good a place as any to start, because as much as we're becoming aware that 'personality' is no longer king when it comes to what defines leadership qualities, we're still floundering for what character traits really matter when it comes to good leadership.

Many other researchers before and since Kiel had tried to identify what characteristics define a good leader of strong character.

In 2004, Dallas-based psychologist Dale Thompson founded Leadership Worth Following with a group of colleagues "in response to what seemed like an epidemic of executive failures of leadership". They created The Worthy Leadership Model, which is rooted in the belief that an accurate leader must encompass three constructs: the capacity to lead, the commitment to lead and the character to lead. In their model, the 'Character to Lead' construct encompasses three factors (personal integrity and ethics; organisational integrity and courage; and humility, gratitude and forgiveness) and nine dimensions (personal integrity, ethics, openness, organisational integrity, courage, power, humility, gratitude and forgiveness).

In a 2007 paper, *The Character of Leadership,* published in the Ivy Business Journal, Cooper et al. write: "We often take the character of leadership for granted. We expect good leaders to be strong in character... These leaders with character have been identified as *authentic* leaders: They are what they believe in; show consistency between their values, ethical reasoning and actions; develop positive psychological states such as confidence, optimism, hope, and resilience in themselves and their associates; and are widely known and respected for their integrity."

The authors ultimately narrow the main traits down to universalism, transformation and benevolence – each of these further broken down into an extensive list of almost 'sub' traits.

We've even had a local study adding to the growing pool of interest and data in character and leadership.

Also published in 2007, *Leadership, Character and its Development* was written by researchers Roslyn De Braine and Derek Verrier. According to the paper, their interest in studying the development of character in leaders was partly inspired by Joseph Badaracco, a professor of Business Ethics at Harvard Business School, who believed that leaders suffer from a "dirty hands problem".

"These and other organisations fall prey to the greed of their leaders in various forms", they write. "This type of leadership crisis partially stems from the crisis of character in individual leaders."

The fallout from this can be extreme. If Keil's -0.57% loss sounds bad, just think of what happened to Enron.

Through an extensive literature review, *Leadership, Character and its Development* reveals that "leadership, integrity, industriousness, empathy, loyalty, optimism, fairness and compassion were considered the most sought-after character elements within leaders in the workplace – and of those, leadership and integrity were the most supported".

And on and on. The interest in leadership and character has been growing since the 1990s, but almost all this conversation has been driven by ethicists, psychologists and organisational researchers behind the scenes, while on stage, personality and skillset have been paraded as the ultimate toolkit of great leadership. Until now. What Kiel and his team surfaced, and what he brought into the spotlight, was this slow rise of awareness that what kind of human you are in business matters to the business. It matters both to your individual success and the humans who work for you *and*, as he demonstrated, to the company's financials. If nothing else, that should be enough to get even the most cynical businessperson listening.

That awareness gained even more momentum shortly after Kiel's book. In 2016, hot on the heels of *Return on Character*, came Angela Duckworth's *Grit: The Power of Passion and Perseverance*. A runaway bestseller, Duckworth drew on her background as a teacher and psychologist to investigate what determines success in both children and adults. Researching output from sources as widely varied as teachers and students at school, to sales floor reps and military academy cadets, Duckworth's theory is that what is most fundamental to success is passion and perseverance – the grit to see things through. Her "grit equation" took the world by storm:

$$\text{Talent x effort = skill}$$
$$\text{Skill x effort = achievement}$$

"Talent is how quickly your skills improve when you invest effort", she says. "Achievement is what happens when you take your acquired skills and use them."

In other words, skill isn't only something you're born with; rather, it's the product of your talent being multiplied by how much effort you put in. Achievement is taking that skill and putting even more effort into it. In her theory, when it comes to success, effort is twice as important as any inherent talent.

"Without effort", she writes, "your skill is nothing more than what you could have done but didn't".

That effort, the perseverance and passion of it, is grit. Duckworth's work on the character trait of grit as a key element to success was, I believe, a watershed moment in the collective awareness of character. It was ground-breaking, easily accessible stuff that dialled up the popular interest in the role that character plays in success, either of the individual or the collective. But there's even greater overlap between her and Kiel – and, indeed, all of the research mentioned above. Because in all these approaches to character, no matter which trait is vaunted over the other, one element stands out: the ability to flex your character muscles.

As Kiel points out, character can be taught.

Flex those muscles

"It dawned on us halfway through this study, that character is mostly a matter of habit. It's not the kind of thing you do a lot of thinking about", says Kiel. "And habits can be changed. Developing character is about strengthening moral habits." Duckworth describes it as building your grit muscle. In fact, she was a cofounder of Character Lab at the time *Grit* hit its stride. As briefly mentioned when talking KIPP, Character Lab is the non-profit organisation founded in 2013 to research and create new ways to help all children and students develop good character traits. Other researchers, like Kiel, talk about forming new habits through repetition and mentorship.

We'll get to more of this later in Part 3, but for now see it as a vital piece of information. Because, as we start unpacking the value of leadership character in effective corporate innovation, it'll be of benefit to know that even if there are elements we feel we might fall short in, it's not lost to us. We can develop the habit, we can build the muscle, and become better leaders building better innovation ecosystems.

The sum of its parts

There's a danger of the book seemingly glorifying some character traits over others. As I mentioned previously, these are simply the leadership traits that, in my experience, directly and positively affect the sustainable, effective, continuous innovation capability of an organisation. It is by no means an exhaustive list, and I plan to research and write about many others in the fullness of time.

I must also emphasise again that no one person can be expected to embody each of these traits to their most glorious potential. Each person is different. Just like some people are built for forging new paths into the future, some people are not. Some people want to be leaders, others just want to do the work and get home by five to unwind. Some people want to be in the mechanic pit, some people want to be in the racing car. And neither is more important than the other. Every person is valuable and necessary in the role they occupy. What we ultimately want is for everyone on the team to be of great character, working towards a collective success.

But that dream team starts with the CEO and their senior leadership teams.

PART 2

CHARACTER: UNPACKING THE DNA OF ORGANISATIONAL INNOVATION

When I started compiling this part of the book, it struck me how basic some of this character stuff is. In fact, it reminded me of Robert Fulghum's *All I Really Need to Know I Learned in Kindergarten*. Some of his rules apply beautifully to how to innovate, essentially as it's related to character.

Some stand outs for me and that feel like they work here are things like 'share everything' (knowledge bases, information, go open source), 'play fair' (don't play favourites, listen to your people), 'clean up your own mess' (telling the truth and proactively taking steps to make amends), 'don't hit people' (be kind, help don't harm, reward and recognise)...

But he's got some other good ones that I want to mention before we dig in with this next part of the book.

'Flush': Learn how to dump the zombie projects and products that are failing. Part of rapid experimentation and solving differently is the capacity to use your resources wisely and with agility. No matter how plush your organisation's bank account, there is no space to waste resources, including people's time at work.

'When you go out into the world, watch out for traffic, hold hands, and stick together': It's all about collaboration. There is no way around it. No individual or collective success happens in a vacuum.

'Be aware of wonder.' Be willing to learn; be open to change and trust and the power of collective problem-solving.

And finally: 'Remember the Dick-and-Jane books and the first word you learned – the biggest word of all – LOOK.' Being a leader who is willing to face the hard truths that come with building innovative thinking into an organisation is essential.

Eric Reis encourages leaders to "celebrate zero as a success" in his *Leader's Guide*. "If you test and the results lead you to zero (growth, interest, customers, change) celebrate that zero as a success", he says. "Replacing the hollow 'wished fors' in your business case with a real, honest-to-goodness 0% is a win – a milestone that establishes the baseline. It's better to have bad news that's true than good news you made up."

I cannot stress enough how much courage it can take for leaders, especially those in legacy organisations, to tell – and not hide – the truth. I imagine it can sometimes feel like that scene from *Birdbox* where Gary forces open Cheryl's eyes to make her see the monsters.

But back to the kindergarten learning. I guess, in short, this is all about not being a jerk. It's about recognising that innovation succeeds when there are good relationships between people of good character; that organisational ecosystems can only adapt to innovative 'future ways of working' if the cultural DNA constructing it is amassed from supportive leadership character traits.

With that being said, what follows are the traits most needed by leadership to realise effective, long-term systems innovative think.

1. Intellectual humility

Innovation doesn't need your ego involved

There's a lot of ego in innovation. I guess there has to be if you're up against a system that likes the status quo and pushes against change. Those who want to create the new often start out as the outsiders of the establishment and have to work hard to assert themselves. But I often wonder if the Silicon Valley image of innovation visionary sometimes tips over into action for the individual's sake, as opposed to the collective good. Maybe that just says something about me, which is probably the best kind of lead-in for this chapter on the character trait of intellectual humility.

Intellectual humility is the capacity to acknowledge that you don't know what you don't know, and that you simply can't know everything. It's the ability to recognise the limitations of your knowledge – and not get defensive, or act against defensiveness, if you're shown up to be wrong. Like most of the traits highlighted in this book, intellectual humility has been, in one form or another, an object of study for philosophers, theologians and psychologists for centuries. Most recently, the capacity for intellectual humility has been linked to cognitive flexibility – the ability to appropriately adjust your behaviour according to your changing environment. In other words, and for our purposes, being able to see the market changes and shifting customer needs, and responding and adapting to those accordingly.

Research has shown that there's a direct link between intellectual humility and an intrinsic motivation to learn, intellectual engagement and open-minded thinking. It's the reason I've chosen to start here, because it's the one trait that is absolutely critical in collaborative work and fundamental for constructive discussions, especially when there are disagreements. It is the basis for innovating in a network and must be present for a growth mindset to take root. It's also closely linked to curiosity, in that it's the first step in wanting to know new information. "What don't I know?" it asks. "Let me find out."

Intellectual humility is the character trait that allows us to acknowledge that we don't know something and that our opinions, beliefs and knowledge base may be wrong. Certainly, in a South African context that is ever-expanding in terms of diversity, the ability to learn from opposing views and consider or take on ideas contrary to your own is imperative. In terms of building the ecosystem that supports sustainable long-term innovative thinking, intellectual humility is defined for me along three streams: the ability to learn, the ability to collaborate and the ability to change.

The ability to collaborate

An important example of the way intellectual humility profoundly affects innovation is the ability to collaborate.

As a leader, this capacity for collaboration manifests in one important way first: abandoning your own personal myth of being a visionary leader. This might sound counter to what might motivate you to be a leader, so maybe a clearer (albeit somewhat longer) statement might read: abandoning your own personal myth of being a visionary leader that creates key person dependency and operates from the HIPPO principle.

Unless you can accept that there are people around you who might know better or who can provide valuable and equally weighted input, you're never going to maximise your team. For any organisation to benefit from innovation practices, it must be something that's baked into the system and owned by the community. What you want for the organisation is to be in almost continuous transformation. In other words, the organisation builds its own rhythm and way of learning that's always on; there's always a team that holds that knowledge base and capacity, and that isn't (and shouldn't be) dependent on any key person. Your one job then as a leader of innovative thinking in the organisation is to make the circle bigger; to set aside the myth of the visionary leader in favour of the leader who inspires the collective by harnessing the wisdom and creative energy of the collective, thereby democratising innovation and making it a long-term culture.

There is simply no space for ego when it comes to organisation-wide innovation success.

Harnessing the power of the collective

I grew up in a mining town in Boksburg. At that time, it was common knowledge that the guys had to go through 10 tons of rubble to get one ounce of gold. Every time I start working with a new group of radical problem solvers in the corporate space I'm reminded of this image because the method I use relies on collective wisdom; the idea that all the voices in the room are smarter than any one or two voices in the room.

The value of the collective in problem-solving is indisputable to me. The more people you bring along in the journey, the more input you can harvest and therefore the greater your chance of finding a solution, that ounce of pure gold, that is not only tailor-made for your organisation but, with all the angles the collective can throw at it, highly evolved.

This is why any process I begin with my clients and their company starts with bringing as many multi-disciplinary stakeholders on board as is possible. And by this I mean bringing everyone involved in the possible scaling along from the outset. Most often, this means bringing in the people from divisions that aren't typically considered sexy. In my experience, the real heroes of innovation are in the back office. They're the Ops people – the ones who have what it takes to successfully plug promising innovations into the core, so that they can stand up and scale. This is where promising innovation goes to die or live. If these people aren't interested or excited, you can't integrate any kind of change and you certainly can't scale it.

Let's say you're a retailer and you're looking to roll out a new process with your floor staff or for your customer experience. Let's say you want to prototype an agile, more streamlined way of working. Beyond the coms and HR guys, your multi-disciplinary team must also comprise line managers and those people who will help you get through the spaghetti of all the functional and admin red tape. These are the people you're going to need to get permission from to run experiments and do things differently; who are going to enable your team through policies and procedures. These people are the thin edge of the wedge – they understand what you need to do and they go get the permissions and deal with the regulatory constraints. They know what's happening on the floor.

They're really where the magic happens and they don't get enough credit. They're quiet heroes. They're the unsexy opposite of the visionary leader. They're not invited to talk at leadership conferences. They don't usually sit at Exco level or on the Board. They're hiding in plain sight.

If senior leadership is unwilling to put their internal status aside for a moment and consider that they and the rest of the executive might not have all the answers, if they don't bring these quiet heroes along because they're beneath the cool kids of the organisation, whatever you put out there, whether it's a product or a process, isn't going to be integrated.

Collaboration requires intellectual humility in leaders to recognise they're not the smartest person in the room simply because they get paid the most. And they're not expected to have all the answers. It's the antidote to the HIPPO mentality, where the highest paid person's opinion wins out. As a leader, the ability to collaborate with everyone and every division, not just the people and functions in your organisation that you find sexy, is an imperative to a culture of continuous transformation and learning to sustainable innovation.

It's how you get buy-in

Getting team buy-in on whatever process you're undertaking is a powerful consequence of using collaboration to harness the power of the collective.

If you're simply using the power of your HIPPO position to force a direction on your team or thrust a new way of working on them, you're going to waste time, money and passion. (There are many ways to expound on each of those – zombie projects gobbling up resources, trashed innovations no one asked for, wasted human potential – but there are other books to delve into those details.) If people show up because they're told to show up – and if there's a whiff of competing politics or ego in the team – you're screwed. If you don't even have alignment on why the process is taking place, you're not going to have alignment on the ideas that come out of it.

Bringing relevant stakeholders along right at the very start of the problem-solving process, even as early as defining or agreeing on the fact that there *is* a problem to solve – that, yes, the boat needs to be steered in a particular direction – will make it easier when it comes to actually cranking those engines to go.

It's how you get alignment

One of the great synergies to watch unfold in Design Thinking workshops is the alignment that slots into place first as people collaborate to understand the problem space and then as they co-create a solution.

To me, the real value isn't always in the solutions that are surfaced, but in this team cohesion that the process inspires. You might come up with a hundred great concepts to improve your service or product for your internal and external customers, but the fact that there's a shared learning and perspective between the stakeholders making it all happen means that everyone will be pulling that big ship in the same direction.

If you form a great team, you're more likely to actually create some implementation magic. Without alignment you have bad to zero implementation. Just think about those quiet heroes who dot all the Is and cross all the Ts and how difficult or easy they can make the realisation of your leadership vision. So for me, the equation looks something like this:

Collaboration leads to co-creation = better alignment = better implementation

You must've heard the adage that goes something like, 'A great idea run by a bad team delivers a terrible result; a good team running with a bad idea can deliver great results.' Because even if the product 'fails', whatever results from the experience will be a step to advanced learnings in future ways of working in the organisation's ecosystem.

And then the real work begins...

Future ways of working are upon us and they require a radical mind shift in what and who leadership is for. It's up to the leader – whether this is a company sanctioned post or a leadership attitude – to pave the way, drive the motivation, explain the 'why', inspire the collective to action. They're also there to keep the ball rolling. Unfortunately, this is where we come to another ego hurdle that intellectual humility can balance out.

Usually, at the start of a process change that is more aligned to an egalitarian input, for instance, leaders find it easy to present themselves as champions of change. The visionary leader is especially eager to create a culture shift that will mark their time as special. But then the ball starts rolling.

While I've found today's HIPPOs to be generally open to the collective solutioning and problem-solving ideation processes, when it becomes clear that this will require actual change to the status quo, they often kick back hard. This is where all those implementation problems I spoke about earlier can mess things up. And if it's senior leadership or legacy systems getting in the way – as it invariably is – I want to tell you a little story I once heard that relates the value of intellectual humility in great leadership...

The ability to change

This is the story of Beowulf. It isn't the literary version, but it'll do for the metaphor.

The story goes that there's a village that's living peacefully and happily until Grendel the dragon appears and starts stealing the odd child and sheep. After a while, the villagers start expecting and accepting this, and the deal is that as long as the dragon takes something only every now and again, everyone's cool. But then Grendel starts returning more often than the villagers think is reasonable. It's eating way beyond its fill and it's starting to be destructive, so they put out a bounty on his head. With that, many warriors arrive to try to slay the dragon but fail.

Of course, there's a prince. His name is Beowulf and naturally, as fairy tales go, he's different to the others. He's not there for the bounty, he's there for the challenge. He slays the dragon, he's the great hero, everyone is thrilled, they start preparing for a big feast ... and then the sky darkens. They look up and it's Grendel's Mom, and boy is she hangry. Because, not only has her son been killed, but Grendel was actually feeding her – and in doing so, keeping her away from the village and its people. She razes the town to the ground, but Beowulf and a couple of his warrior mates manage to survive.

The crisis now gets escalated to the King's Council and they adjust the bounty, attracting many more warriors from afar. However, Grendel's Mom lives in an air-pocketed lake in the mountains. When the warriors arrive and stand at the edge of the lake they realise that they're not prepared. All the things that they've been trained to use to slay a dragon no longer work. If they want to get to her, they have to leave their horses behind and shed all their steel armour and swords on the shore, because if they take any of it they'll drown for sure.

But, hurrah! Our hero Beowulf saves the day. He is the only one brave enough to be vulnerable, to shed all his known methods of attack and to jump into the lake naked and barehanded. He ends up slaying the giant dragon in a tussle, by slashing her throat with her own talon. The end.

To me, this is the perfect metaphor of innovation in the age of modernising the organisation for future ways of working, and a powerful image of the process we see unfold in deep organisational development. I first heard it from a mentor of mine, Craig Yeatman, the longstanding chairman of the South African Organisation Development Network (SAODN), at a SAODN training programme he was delivering. The translation goes something like this...

Grendel often appears as, 'We're not customer-centric enough – let's restructure' or 'We're not digital enough, let's embrace exponential technologies and New Ways of Working'.

The call is put out to the organisation, the teams are rallied, the weapons are assembled, and then they start looking at that problem. At the start of the process, it always seems to be going well – the team thinks it's solving the problem, they think they've won. They're empathising with the customer, they're prototyping, they're surfacing how new ways of working that can drive the business forward and be better for the people. It's all going great. The dragon is slayed! All the team needs now is some deep systems change or flex and the resources to implement this, so they turn to leadership. And then comes the real problem. Enter Grendel's mother.

The team finds that the real problem is actually sitting deeper down and broader across, and all the more problematic: their real problem wasn't that they needed a new product or an admin process. Their problem is a cultural issue on the inside that will kick against systems change. And that cultural issue looks like leadership pushback, often by the very leaders who asked for the change in the first place.

Grendel's Mom – leadership and the status quo

Many informed leaders want to present themselves as being on the cutting edge of business. It suits their egos and profile to be the ones to suggest new ways of working that are cognisant of market shifts and future needs, so they're often the ones asking for the organisation to innovate more and modernise.

But they learn very quickly that in new ways of working, you're sourcing the people's collective wisdom and that it's not the highest paid person's opinion that matters most. They might start finding that the data contradict their smartest person's one good idea or reveal that the solutions they championed are not the solutions wanted or needed by the customer. They might come to the realisation that a beloved zombie project needs to be cut.

Finally, at some point, they start realising the implications of handing over some of their discretionary decision-making rights and not being the most important person around. They face the fact that modernising is a call for leaders to become genuine servant leaders – that their purpose is to remove obstacles and provide air cover for others to shine. They find that the customer, both internal and external, is genuinely central and must get served before anyone else; that leaders are served second and only when they've proven their contribution (not this basically state-sanctioned bullshit of getting bonuses and huge salaries when the company they're tasked to lead is crumbling).

Often, it's the CEO and/or executive team who are most resistant. Many big legacy corporates are run by big egos who simply don't want things done differently. Their unspoken change management philosophy is simple: 'Fit in or fuck off.' It doesn't matter what they say to win the hearts and minds of their people. When it comes down to it, they will choose to secure the stability of their own futures instead of that of the business. (And why not? It's not *their* business, after all.)

Of course, resistance to supporting change can be true for anyone in a leadership position and this isn't just about ego versus intellectual humility. This is about a culture of fear and risk aversion that pervades legacy corporations. Most leaders pushing back don't want things to change because change means risking not only their position but threatening the short-term stability of the organisation. Every move in a new direction is stopped by: 'Could this be grounds for getting me fired?' There are a lot of parties complicit in this kind of scenario.

Grendel's Mom isn't just the ego-based, protectionist leader in the organisation. The shareholders of these listed companies, the government and even provinces, don't really want the status quo to change. They don't really want these big companies disrupted. They want a clear and obvious line of sight on their books: we're making this much tax or return out of X company and we want to be able to bank on that.

So people in leadership positions often want to protect their empires as is. Apart from the obvious pushbacks during implementation – cutting off resources, cutting short the prototyping, simply dropping the ball – I've also noticed Grendel's Mom creeping into the process right at the start.

For example, when Exco members are asked to shortlist their brightest and best to start the process, they consciously or unconsciously send the problem children or the B team players; passengers in the organisation who know the boundaries are low on accountability so they just play the system. And sometimes problem children are great. They're often people who are so frustrated by the bureaucracy that they present as problematic but many are incredible agents of change. But, that's rare. So sending in the B-team because you feel you can risk their time investment becomes an act of sabotage.

Which is why invitations to apply for any innovation process and recruitment into the process is so powerful and helps level the playing field. The people who go through the effort not only display grit and intrinsic motivation, but the intellectual humility to accept the challenge. I've seen on these kinds of projects where top people are asked to come in to be part of this and they arrive with indifference and arrogance. It affirms and recognises them in the wrong way.

Grendel's Mom is the people around the leadership table. Since culture is driven by the leadership team, if they are a bunch of short-termist, bonus-taking executives, managers or bureaucrats, they're going to negatively affect that culture and the organisation's capacity to respond and get agile. Ultimately, systemic change can never come from the custodians of the status quo; they're not going to be the turkeys that vote for Christmas lunch. Therefore, for real change to happen, theirs is the short-term mindset that needs to be slayed.

Taking off the armour

Beowulf is such a perfect metaphor for leadership in the innovation process because it's not just about the person who is willing to challenge the status quo and the deep systems, but who is willing to remove the armour of traditional leadership, the sword of all-knowing authority and slay what needs to be slayed in order to protect and strengthen the organisation. When Beowulf goes to the lake, the hero immediately understands that the old ways of killing dragons isn't going to work. She or he knows that what got us here isn't going to get us there.

Intellectual humility is the cognitive flexibility and intelligence to know that there are things you don't know. Julia Cameron, author of the bestseller *Artist's Way*, calls it the grace to be a beginner. "The grace to be a beginner is always the best prayer for an artist. The beginner's humility and openness lead to exploration. Exploration leads to accomplishment. All of it begins at the beginning, with the first small and scary step..." You might not consider yourself an artist, but innovation in any form is the act of breaking new ground. It is the act of getting comfortable with the vulnerability of not knowing – of making mistakes.

To allow yourself as a leader to pave the way for your organisation's success by tapping into the collective instead of trying to do it all yourself or push your own agenda requires intellectual humility. It requires a leader who is willing to think differently and who wants to slay Grendel's Mom, that great cultural barrier to organisational change.

The ability to learn

The ability to learn is premised at some level on intellectual humility; you need to recognise and acknowledge that there are things you do not know. In the face of conflicting evidence to what you hold to be true, you need to be open to changing your opinions. I must admit, this is a near-impossible ask. Studies upon studies have been conducted into the problem of confirmation bias – or what's now being referred to as 'myside bias' – and the fact that facts don't change our minds. But for innovative thinking to flourish, it's a muscle you're going to have to strengthen.

In any innovation process that involves prototyping or experimentation, you need to be able to accept the data even if they contradict your viewpoint; in empathy work for the customer, you need to be able to put your biases aside; in collective and collaborative work, you need to be able to detach from your personal story and hold it lightly as you engage with people from diverse backgrounds, knowledge bases and skillsets. When it comes to prototyping there is humility in recognising that you're probably going to, in a very messy way, pick the wrong fight before the real issue emerges in the organisation. There's humility in accepting that how you've been taught to deal with that issue is probably not going to work; that you're going to have to embrace a whole new bunch of ways of working that you'll be a novice at – that you'll feel very vulnerable about.

Will you have the humility to give yourself the grace to be a beginner and deal with the real issues? It takes a particular kind of leader to embrace this.

It's all spaghetti

No matter how much we try to dissect the process and outcomes of innovation neatly under a surgical light, every organisation, every team, every individual going through the process of adapting – and learning to adapt – to new ways of working and thinking will come at the process differently. The tweaks will be different, the needs will be different. The cultural baseline of the leadership character will vary. We must accept that it's complex and ambiguous and stop burning fuel trying to understand it fully.

Dr Michael Kahn said it best at a STI presentation I went to in 2019. Khan is Extraordinary Professor in the Centre for Research on Evaluation, Science and Technology at Stellenbosch University, and a member of the DST-NRF Centre of Excellence in Scientometrics and Science Policy. After he'd presented a whole piece of indications and insights into making everything work, he just loaded a picture of a bowl of spaghetti onto the screen.

This is what innovation is, he said. It's not neat, everything's connected and all these things matter to each other.

I'm paraphrasing loosely, but that was the gist of it. We can be academic about it and pontificate on this in relation to that. We can try to disentangle the process and come at it in a linear fashion. We can try to put people and departments into their silos. We can spend all our time on one strand of spaghetti at the detriment of the rest of the bowl. But this would be futile and, ultimately, arrogant.

No leader has all the answers. No leader knows exactly how the process of becoming or adapting for an innovation-minded ecosystem will unfold. Everything can only be guided and supported and adapted to as new information arises. There is no controlling it.

There is humility in accepting this. It just is what it is. Just fork up the delicious, tasty mess of it and learn as you go.

2. Grit

How purpose and perseverance affect your innovation game

What I loved about Ducksworth's *Grit* was that it helped to further define, in a very accessible, broad-based, non-sector specific manner, success as the product of character. Her hypothesis that the secret to outstanding achievement is not talent but grit really struck me. For one thing, it's relieving to know that success isn't hinged solely on skill or talent or privilege linked to cosmic luck. After all, there's more possibility and scope for the average, non-genius Joe like me. But beyond my own small thrill at that, it's her breakdown of grit into its constituent parts that its importance as a leadership trait supporting effective corporate innovation becomes especially clear.

Grit, in Duckworth's equation, is 'passion' plus 'perseverance' for long-term goals. Passion and perseverance are familiar terms in start-up and legacy businesses. They're bandied about relentlessly in start-up culture and innovation conversations, and they're favourites for visionary leaders trying to trail-blaze their way through this arena. In corporate spaces, the value of 'passion' as an emotive quality linked to the organisation's people – employees, customers, business stakeholders – is increasingly recognised as a powerful ingredient in driving motivation or energy for projects at hand. Certainly, perseverance in the face of multiple failures is considered one of the defining experiences of entrepreneurial spirit.

But what struck me was Duckworth's interpretation of passion and perseverance and how deeply connected they are. Perseverance is no longer driven by willpower but by passion. Passion itself is not some poetic flamboyance of spirit. Passion, she explains, comprises its own constituent parts of 'interest' and 'purpose'. Without these two elements working together to create passion for a goal, she says, there's no reason to get up and try, try again if your first, second or seventh attempts fail; there's no reason to persevere.

While I love the word 'passion', what feels more connected to the innovation space is the 'purpose' element of it. Intrapreneurs and leaders actively supporting new ways of working and future spaces are already, by definition, high in interest. What we're looking at is what drives that interest and how. I believe that thriving 21st century organisations have three elements in common:

1. They're committed to a purpose beyond profit.
2. They choose to take a long-term view.
3. They continuously produce profitable solutions to the problems of people and planet.

Creating agile organisations embodying all three elements requires leaders who are fluent in patience, discipline and restraint. I believe these are qualities best exemplified by the grit character trait, and in particular its elements of purpose and perseverance.

Purpose: The intrinsic motivation that drives innovation

Purpose, the idea of fulfilling one's full potential and greater good, has been fodder for thinky types for centuries. Aristotle used the Greek term *'telos'* to refer to the inherent purpose of a person or object. Cicero wrote of it as "the highest, ultimate or final Good" and that "the Chief Good is to live agreeably". In Duckworth's interpretation, purpose is the intention to contribute to the well-being of others.

It's important to be clear about what purpose is, because grittiness and a passion for something are certainly not the properties only of those who wish to leave a positive legacy for their community, country or the world. As Duckworth points out, Stalin and Hitler were gritty. From my point of view, Donald Trump certainly had grit, as do Putin and the evil nerds down at Facebook and Amazon. Ditto the criminals who lead the auditing firms and management consultancies that helped corrupt members of Parliament achieve state capture in South Africa – during and post-apartheid. But these kinds of people and organisations are not the ones signing up to modernise their businesses by becoming more human-centric in all the best possible ways. Their personal motivating energy isn't necessarily one shared and supported by, or inspiring to, their collective workforce. Which is okay. Others are on it. As Duckworth says: "There may be gritty villains in the world, but my research suggests there are many more gritty heroes."

I'll take a guess that quite a lot of these gritty heroes are sitting in your workforce and, since you're reading this book, I'm going to assume that you're one of them or aiming to be one of them. In my mind, that makes you part of the leadership group that wants to leave a positive legacy or, at very least, do some good while they're around. Looking at the literature and collectives that have been emerging on the outskirts of traditional business practice since the early 2000s – and starting to creep in and influence that space – there's a clear, widespread impulse to do better for the betterment of everyone. 'Purpose' as a motivating factor is coming in from the fringe.

In his book *Purpose: The Starting Point of Great Companies*, Nikos Mourkogiannis goes into depth about the power of purpose as it effects leadership and drives organisational action. He published the book in 2008, at a time when trust in corporate structures was going through a global wobble. "I believe that Purpose – not money, not status – is what people most want from work", writes Mourkogiannis. "Make no mistake: They want compensation; some want an ego-affirming title. Even more, though, they want their lives to mean something, they want their lives to have a reason."

A year later, in 2009, Simon Sinek introduced his big 'why' concept at a TED Talk, speaking to this first kernel of popular business interest in purpose work and how it affects marketability. "People don't buy what you do; they buy why you do it", was the basic gist of his talk and subsequent book, *Start with Why: How Great Leaders Inspire Everyone to Take Action*. Both thought leaders (and indeed, many others beating the same drum) were ahead of a generational curve.

In 2020, New York-based communications agency Zeno Group released the findings of their global study into brands and purpose, and confirmed what the likes of Mourkogiannis and Sinek have been saying for years: A leader and business' purpose now affects not just their current and future employee base, but their consumer base.

Their 'Strength of Purpose' study included 8,000 consumers across eight countries and four languages, and evaluated more than 75 brands, revealing that global consumers are "four to six times more likely to trust, buy, champion and protect those companies with a strong purpose over those with a weaker one".

Speaking to *Forbes* about the findings, Alison DaSilva, Managing Director of Purpose and Impact at Zeno, said: "Consumers have raised the bar and are looking to companies to advance progress on important issues within and outside of their operational footprint. Globally, 94% of consumers said it is important that the companies they engage with have a strong Purpose, and 83% said companies should only earn a profit if they also deliver a positive impact."

Leading the charge on this are the younger generations – the Millennials and GenZs. Looking at that trajectory of growing social consciousness, one can assume that the upcoming Alphas will be no different. Zeno's findings gel with those coming out of McKinsey. In a 2021 report, *The Diversity Imperative in Retail*, one particular quote stands out for me: "Almost 40 percent of millennials have not pursued or have turned down a job because they perceived their potential employer to lack inclusive mindsets and actions. More than half of people of colour (52 percent) will not work for a company that fails to speak out on racial inequality."

This is your current and future employee base. Even if you believed making money was your company's purpose, your future money-making platforms will be urging you to think otherwise. It doesn't mean that your organisation has to stand for saving the issues of the world, but it must stand for something that amounts to more than supporting a form of capitalism that simply extracts.

This might leave public legacy organisations or established private companies in the dwang if they haven't figured this stuff out. Often, older companies haven't formulated or discovered their purpose from the get-go (after all, wasn't the purpose to make money?) or haven't updated it from the hand-me-downs scribbled on a napkin from the founders who built the company and were driven by their own purpose – founders who have long since left. Other organisations find themselves in a terminology Gordian knot between 'vision' (where you're going), 'mission' (for whom), 'values' (how you plan to get there) and 'purpose' (why you're going), and attempt to find purpose by clarifying the vision and the mission, or laying out the strategy. But this is a bit backwards. If you don't know why you're going somewhere, why bother with going or how you get there?

So, as per Sinek's catchy phrase: "Start with the why." Once you have that in place, says Mourkogiannis, an effective purpose "will not simply translate into goals, it will also stimulate and guide actions in the firm that are not specified in this formal way, illuminating and guiding day-to-day interactions with customers and colleagues".

His book is a worthwhile read for organisations and leaders looking to broaden their understanding of purpose. There are many, of course, but for our intentions, purpose's animating energy for innovation should be clear: without the why of it – the originating force, the reason for action – innovation is simply pushing fancy toys around the table to amuse a senior exec or throw darts around in R&D. And this is not just at an individual leadership level. Purpose, the intrinsic motivation that drives follow-through, is something you need for the entire team, division or company if you're going to inspire your people for the project at hand.

'It's what gets me out of bed in the morning.'

I've been privileged to work with major corporations that have used the power of their purpose to drive the build not only of innovative products and services, but the organisation's agility and innovation ecosystem. However, one of all my all-time favourite stories comes from the start-up space.

Yoco, a South African fintech start-up turned fully fledged business, made its name as a supplier of card payment devices to the SME market, traditionally a section excluded from the banking system, democratising access to payment solutions for South African entrepreneurs.

The story goes that in 2011, cofounder Katlego Maphai found himself at a hole-in-the-wall barbecue eatery in San Francisco. At the end of the meal, he noticed that there was no cash box or till in sight, and no card machine. When it came time to pay, the owner whipped out her old Android phone, took his credit card and slipped it into a small device attached to her phone. Payment was made, easy as pie.

Maphai took the idea back to his cofounders and over time it developed into the business that is Yoco today. They've since branched out to build tools and services to help small businesses do better business at scale. Their underlying purpose, says Maphai, is to enable people and communities to thrive. "This is what gets us up in the morning; this is what we do", he says.

Before Yoco, like every entrepreneur, Maphai and his friends had been looking at a wide range of projects to work on, even landing briefly on the idea of a wine bar.

"But we were attracted to entrepreneurship to make a difference. We really took on this idea that your gain doesn't have to be somebody else's loss. That's very dated thinking, all predicated on scarcity. This idea that we could build a company where our customers doing well represented us doing well and vice versa was something that resonated very deeply with us. We weren't just building a successful organisation, but actually challenging how organisations are built and the role they play within society, breaking down the walls between your customers, your team, your community... everyone's plugged in."

As the idea of Yoco slowly emerged through their research and the exploration of its possibility, and as it was built, so their purpose came to life.

"The sense of connectedness that we can all collectively thrive, that nobody has to lose in the process is, for me, probably one of the most transformational ideas that exists within the company."

Yoco wasn't their purpose, it was simply the best vehicle for their purpose. Today it's the largest independent mobile point-of-sale player in the country, with more than 5,000 merchants in South Africa.

"I see myself as no different to one of our merchants – we're all a small business, we're all business owners and entrepreneurs, struggling with the same things and it's such a privilege to have that level of kinship with your customers."

Collective purpose in the corporate innovation space

The kind of alignment that we might see in a start-up such as Yoco around a common purpose in driving whatever innovation is theirs, is not impossible to create in large organisations. Sure, the levers are different and the ecosystem broader, more established and slower to turn towards a common goal, but it is possible. And it simply must be, because corporate innovation needs alignment to work – alignment between team members, between leadership and employees, between leadership and Exco. I've already spoken about the value of collaboration in building this alignment, but creating alignment starts even before any of the problem-solving processes do. It starts in the same place that start-ups like Yoco do: with purpose.

Mourkogiannis talks a lot about purpose and it's interaction with and value to innovation. What I love about it is how he connects this to relationships:

"Purpose also reduces risk aversion and fear and helps innovators see beyond current convention. It underpins trust between individuals both within and beyond the firm, as well as making individuals more sensitive to each other's requirements. In these ways, Purpose stimulates the two key forms of action that contribute to the strengths of the firm and thus competitive advantage – innovation and the formation of relationships. These forms of action constantly refresh the firm's strengths, creating an enduring advantage that is not dependent on the fate of this or that strategic position."

When I start work with a team, where we're looking at any kind of innovation work – whether it's a radical problem-solving process, prototyping or embracing new ways of working – I most often start with the challenge framing process found in Design Thinking.

The size of the team I kick off with varies wildly. It could start with the leader or leadership team of two or four initiating the project, or with a group of 70 people from seven different business units across the organisation. Whoever the process starts off with, the starting point is the same: aligning around the purpose of why we're in the room together.

This is ultimately what 'framing the challenge' means. It's about finding and framing the most pressing problem that the team in the room is looking to solve, and agreeing on what that is. Often it's not the same problem they thought they were bringing to the table. Sometimes, each individual in the collective has their own unique view on what that problem is. Very often, what is initially presented is merely a symptom masquerading as a problem or an executive's pet project. Almost always, the problem is something deeper and broader than what was initially thought.

We unpack the problem by asking questions such as: 'Who are the people we're solving for?', 'What do they feel and need?', 'Why do they need this change?' and so on. In exploring the problem space, we are in effect finding the purpose around which the team can rally and align.

Whatever ends up surfacing, the challenge framing process pulls the collective together to focus on a common purpose. It aligns language, meaning and motivation, so that the team is pointed in the same direction. This can be particularly daunting in a complex and established organisation, where hierarchies are entrenched and divisions often siloed, but I haven't yet found a better way as an entry point to any problem-solving process.

Galvanising purpose goes beyond just kicking off from the innovation starting blocks. Collective buy-in on a change motivates and inspires people to affect it. It drives grittiness and supports the team and change agents to push through the difficult aspects of innovation and modernising.

"Purpose is a tremendously powerful source of motivation", writes Duckworth. "There may be exceptions, but the rarity of these exceptions proves the rule."

Global consulting firms from Deloitte to EY are pumping out reports and research confirming the effect that purpose has not only on business success, but on innovation. A great read on this for me is *The Business Case for Purpose*, a 2015 report by EY's Beacon Institute in collaboration with *Harvard Business Review*. There's a quote in the findings that sums it up perfectly for me. It's by Rebecca Henderson, an economist, professor at Harvard Business School and author of *Reimagining Capitalism*.

"The sense of being part of something greater than yourself can lead to high levels of engagement, high levels of creativity, and the willingness to partner across functional and product boundaries within a company, which are hugely powerful", she's quoted as saying. "Once they're past a certain financial threshold, many people are as motivated by intrinsic meaning and the sense that they are contributing to something worthwhile as much as they are by financial returns or status."

And this is before Covid and the social consciousness movements that started gaining ground in 2020. It's something that Mourkogiannis said more than a decade ago, which others have pointed out before him, but I love how people are converging on the same idea no matter what road they're taking: whether its innovation for business success and revenue growth, leadership effectiveness, individual meaning, collective growth, or reimagining economic and organisational systems.

Into the future

When you lead your team into an innovation process, when you envision your business with agility and a supporting ecosystem, you must first think about why this change is imperative for you, your team and the health of your organisation. The leadership team needs to buy into it. Your people need to buy into it. We are long past the format of the top-down leadership directive of 'just do what I say'. Sure, there are businesses that still operate that way, workers who prefer that and managers who need that, but I don't believe this is the way our future looks. New generations ask 'why' and expect to be answered and find meaning in that answer.

There are myriad processes that can help you and the company discover what that purpose is. If you haven't done it yet, start. Mine is to help people protect and nurture their creativity. This hasn't been easy given the platforms life has led me to. But then it's not easy to serve a purpose, because when the 'why' becomes clear, the next obvious inflation is around the 'what' and the 'how'. This can be daunting for the individual as much as the organisation.

But I believe that being able to foster the character trait of grittiness driven by purpose is a leadership quality that will be required in the 21st century. It will be required from leaders because it will be required from business and the people who make business work. The deeper we move into the new, and the greater the consciousness around our collective corporate responsibility to the humans and the environment around us grows, the more I believe purpose work will become an imperative for legacy organisations looking to modernise – and by that I mean creating an effective and agile problem-solving, innovative ecosystem able to respond to the market and optimise the creative talents of its people.

Perseverance: The time and patience for taking the long view

There's a cartoon about perseverance that you must've seen by now. It's the one where the guy's digging a tunnel with a pick-axe and he's been going at it for months. It's hard slog through the rock and the dirt and the dude's tired as hell. You see him work through the tunnel over about three or four frames, getting nowhere, just hitting more and more rock and dirt. Eventually, he stops. It's just taken too long to find what he's looking for and it's time to give up. In the last frame, you see him walking away from the narrow wall of dirt he was just about to break through if he'd just kept going – and the diamond stash on the other side.

So close, yet so very far.

Steve Jobs once said: "I'm convinced that about half of what separates the successful entrepreneurs from the non-successful ones is pure perseverance. It is so hard."

If grit is passion (interest and purpose) and perseverance for long-term goals, then success can only be achieved by pressing through the complexities, the obstacles and the failures – time and time again. Duckworth likes to quote the Japanese saying: 'Fall seven times, stand up eight.'

When I started talking to Maphai about the purpose behind Yoko, the perseverance part of the grit equation became immediately clear.

"We weren't the only ones looking at this model", he says. "The difference was that the other guys just didn't have the patience."

Maphai showed me a graph of user uptake since 2014, when the company became operational with their first 10 transactions. The official launch was in 2015, but user engagement only really kicks off and accelerates hard from 2016, after which the line ticks up in impressive leaps. By the start of 2020, what began almost a decade earlier with an idea, is finally hitting its stride.

And then there's that shocking drop.

"COVID-19. It was scary as hell. We basically went back down to 2016 volumes. It felt like we went backwards."

Luckily, the end of the drop is the bottom of a trench where the line shoots up again and the company rebounds stronger than before.

"I've been staring at this picture for a few days now." Maphai pauses for a moment. "It's like the heartbeat of the company over a long period of time. This is the story of patience. We think really long term. Doing so just allows you the space to better deal with these blips and things going wrong because you inherently believe in the long-term viability of the business and that you just gotta ride it out."

Perseverance is the difference between experiencing a set-back as an outright failure in the short-term and experiencing it as a bump in the road on a long-term journey. It's the heartbeat on that graph; the physical manifestation of time and patience: time to get perspective on the process and the patience to give the process time. Without it, the risk of the new will feel too daunting and any innovation will struggle to survive. Perseverance is the capacity to 'see beyond'. More on that later.

Leadership and perseverance

In the early days, when we used to think about the archetypal innovator's personality, we would think of them as innately curious ideas-people; visionaries always looking to the horizon. But now we know that the reality is a lot less glamorous. Great innovators are the people who keep going, who have the patience to persevere; to keep on keeping on, pushing through the discomfort, leaning into the difficult learning, getting up when they fall down. In my mind, grit is the bedrock of implementation.

Local innovation hero Michael Jordaan used to like to point out that you can have great ideas, but if they're not implemented they're worth nothing. Without the grit to implement, fancy ideas go nowhere. If you've got high curiosity but low grit, you're not going to be a great innovator. As a leader, if you don't have the patience, the perseverance, to stand by your team as they work through the problem-solving, if you can't provide them the air cover and the continuity, if you don't have the persistence in building trust in and between the people you've asked to do this work, then you're not going to be able to build that ecosystem that can support long-term, sustainable innovation. It's not about smartness and glamour; it's about being intrinsically motivated to just push through all the shit.

When we talk about building the ecosystem to support innovation in modernising organisations and systems, this is about the long-term context. This is particularly true of the corporate space. Innovation tools and processes such as Lean and Agile might promise that you'll move at speed, but if you're in a corporate environment, where everything is constipated, politicised and risk-averse, it doesn't matter how good your handle on these methodologies are, you're not going to move at speed. Problematically, legacy organisations don't always have the patience to recognise their inherent slowness either, or the leadership motivation to change this.

It's easier to show you the value that perseverance plays in corporate innovation by showing you the damage its opposing forces – short-termism and impatient investors – can do to kill any kind of innovation at any level.

1.   Short-termism kills funding and resources

It might seem counterintuitive to the whole 'think fast, move fast' philosophy of the early 'innovation is king' drive, but perseverance – time and patience – is a fundamental aspect of innovative thinking and innovating well, whether you're going for a product, service or systems overhaul. And yet, time and patience are two of the resources most lacking and, I believe, misunderstood when it comes to the perceived benefits of building an innovation ecosystem.

Eric Ries, one of the most influential thought leaders and drivers of new innovation practice in the industry today, tackles the problem of time, value and innovation in his book *The Leader's Guide to Adopting Lean Start-up At Scale*. "Innovation projects with promising, but highly uncertain, futures are ranked against legacy products whose projected ROI is a lot easier to predict", he says.

When pitching your idea, whether it's a prototype for a product or a streamlined process for an internal customer, you're going to come up face first against the immediacy of the bottom line. The result? You'll struggle to get the resources you need – the time, money and people – to follow through on your project or even get it started. But, he says (and I love his take on this): "Measuring the ROI of an MVP is a bit like measuring an acorn and cutting off its water supply because it's not yet a tree."

I lived this lack of patience and perseverance most poignantly when I was heading up the innovation capability build at one of major banks, and those 'close the gap' teams would arrive with a mandate from the CEO to close the gap on the income statement. These guys would basically walk around the office and go: "What are you doing? An innovation?! Stop that right now, jump on the phone and sell these fucking credit cards."

And that's just what front-line innovators had to put up with. No dedicated time, patience or respect for the long-term process. Innovation often gets killed in the wake of short-term pressures to deliver financial performance and pay the execs and shareholders their fat bonuses every quarter (more on that in a bit). This is fairly common practice. It's bad enough when this sort of thing happens in a product innovation space, but what happens when you're looking at modernising a service or a work process? These are systems that take time to prototype, test, iterate, integrate through buy-in and change management, and then scale. Taking a short-term view on hard cash savings on this process simply isn't viable.

In these particularly uncertain economic times, it's even more difficult to convince an Exco or the Board to see the value of innovating and to set aside resources for these processes, especially those that aim to institute new ways of working. In this case, there isn't even necessarily a product that can be held in your hands and sold on to a customer. There's no solid prediction of success or easily defined ROI. In *Leader's Guide*, Ries goes some way to adjusting the view on what value is and how to measure it while undertaking an innovation project. Ultimately, he says, it's about shifting perspective to see the value in learning what works and what doesn't, so that you can figure out what matters to your customers (both internal and external) faster than what your competitors do. When you're in the process of modernising your business, for example, you help your teams build trust, you teach them to collaborate, and you learn how to inspire intrinsic motivation and use your resources and people more effectively. You strengthen your workforce with the skillsets of agility and human-centred problem-solving. You practice prototyping and streamlining and building a business that can shift and move with the times.

The learning here is almost infinite, but none of that happens overnight. It takes a leader with the time, patience and perseverance to munch through the messy spaghetti of it. It might not be the sexy image of a Silicon Valley innovation superstar that we've all come to expect from our visionary leaders, but that's what's needed. It reminds me of Malcolm Gladwell's *Revisionist History* podcast episode Puzzle Rush and its sequel. He argues that traits such as being super-conscientious, even neurotic, can be incredibly valuable and highly suited in jobs that require mastering complex problems. Why then, he asks, do we design Lean and Agile innovation practices that are biased against people with these character traits, especially when they are innovating to solve a complex problem?

2. Short-termism can't handle a portfolio

Portfolio balancing is a strategic tool used by innovators to plot and analyse the long- and short-term risk of innovation projects in their pipeline. This is the Three Horizons Framework I spoke about earlier, which outlines how businesses should invest in three different types of innovations, namely Horizon 1 (core), Horizon 2 (adjacent) and Horizon 3 (transformational).

Horizon 1 is 70% of innovation activity to low-risk projects (knowns such as process improvements that'll deliver incremental benefit at scale within a year). Horizon 2 is 20% to moderately risky projects, such as new products and services within a known sector that'll deliver growing benefits over a two-to-three-year time horizon. And Horizon 3 is 10% to high-risk projects, such as moon shots within unfamiliar or invented sectors that may deliver benefits over a much longer period. As I said, the framework initially included time horizons, but these have been dropped since the rate at which we can innovate using modern technology just keeps increasing.

There are various interpretations of this matrix, but basically the bottom line is common: It forces us to look up from our balance sheets of now and ask 'What next?' It takes the long view while allowing for managed risk. It's a 'safe' way for legacy organisations hoping to future-proof themselves to manage innovation strategically and allow space to play with risk in a contained manner, while focusing on a solid supply of quick wins that build trust, not just in the process but in the greater business. Oxford professor Colin Mayer, author of *Prosperity: Better Business Makes the Greater Good*, shows that this kind of ongoing value creation builds trust. This is a key unlock for supporting innovation and I'll go into this in more detail later, but for now it's enough to say that trust results in more loyal customers, more engaged employees, more supportive shareholders and, ultimately, higher revenues and lower costs.

Portfolio balancing for innovation in incumbents is, I believe, a good response to the work of Harvard professor Clayton Christensen. In 1997, Christensen released what would be a ground-breaking treatise on innovation called *The Innovator's Dilemma: When New Technologies Cause Great Firms to Fail*. It sought to explain why successful incumbents led by conscientious managers still manage to lose market leadership to disruptors. By following the very processes that make these organisations successful – focusing only on the current customer base, keeping tight purse strings, focusing on what is known, being risk averse – they fail to prepare for what's next. Think of what happened to the likes of Nokia and Kodak.

It reminds me of the incredible success Capitec has seen in South Africa. Typically, incumbents don't care about or ignore an existing market they can't figure out how to service profitably, and they certainly don't seek them out as part of a long-term strategy. Most often this ignored segment ends up being poorer demographics and micro-enterprises. Capitec was the perfect disruptor, coming along to fish in the pond but focusing on the customers the incumbents didn't know how to service. By using emerging technology to capture this neglected customer base, they were also more efficient, cost-effective and agile – making their service suddenly very attractive to all customers, including the incumbent's long-term clients. It's why I can sit in a Capitec bank surrounded by both the wealthiest and poorest in the country. The incumbents haven't been able to keep up. Given the parameters constraining big organisations, this slow to no response should almost be expected.

"Successful companies want their resources to be focused on activities that address [existing] customers' needs that promise higher profits, that are technologically feasible, and that help them play in substantial markets", explains Christensen. "Yet, to expect the processes that accomplish those things also to do something like nurturing disruptive technologies – to focus resources on proposals that customers reject, that offer lower profit, that underperform existing technologies and can only be sold in insignificant markets – is akin to flapping one's arms with wings strapped to them in an attempt to fly."

To expect this, he says, is to fight the fundamentals of how successful organisations work and how their performance is evaluated.

In short, the innovator's dilemma is that even though you as an incumbent might see the need for change, the system is set up to view ROI and the existing customer base as sacrosanct. The result? Grendel's Mom comes roaring out, rejecting investment in the new under the auspices of company risk versus company fiduciary interests.

A truly successful and effective company needs managers who know how and when to abandon traditional business practices and in service to what purpose.

Now, more than two decades after *Innovator's Dilemma* was published, I think we're getting to a point where big organisations are understanding that those traditional business practices need to catch a wake-up call. And not just on the product development front. The culture surrounding legacy organisations needs to start slowly shifting to agility with a long-term view to better respond to the market and prepare for future customers and employee bases. Leaders can and should be held accountable for managing a balanced portfolio of opportunities – it's irresponsible not to be taking a little bit of risk.

The Long-Term Stock Exchange

Ries' take on organisations and how they operate around innovation is so transformative that his Startup Way work at GE seems to have contributed directly or indirectly to the then GE Chairman and CEO Jeffrey Immelt and Vice Chair Beth Comstock both getting fired. It's difficult not to be inspired by this guy. So when I read about his Long-Term Stock Exchange or LTSE in *The Lean Startup* I couldn't let the idea go.

Ries proposes the idea of an LTSE – a public market designed for trading the stocks of companies organised to sustain long-term thinking. The LTSE isn't aimed at start-ups, but is rather a challenger to stock exchanges. Instead of founders having to do that deal with the devil to raise cash to scale, they go to the LTSE to find patient investors. Its objective is to be a better option for innovative companies to access the public markets, where shareholders understand the value of patience.

In his research for *The Lean Startup,* Ries came to understand the detrimental impact of short-termism not just on innovation, but as a threat to value creation and the health of companies and the market in general, as focus became increasingly centred on the erratic nature of the stock market.

Writing about this on his blog, Ries says: "Public company CEOs and managers shared stories about entire workforces becoming entranced by the pendulum swings of their stock price. They spoke of the challenge of keeping employees focused on the long-term mission while the markets and financial media relentlessly commented on immediate results. They expressed deep regret about starting to play the guidance game. They spoke of the pressure to manage to Wall Street vanity metrics instead of the leading indicators that drive future growth."

Ultimately, the now random rise and fall of stock markets too significantly and negatively impacts the choices companies make on the floor of their business. We just have to look at the mess of GameStop in 2021, when a Reddit forum took out Wall Street for a few days to see how dangerous it is to peg strategy to stocks.

As Ries points out: "If the stock dropped a point, was that random volatility, or a signal that large investors were losing faith in the company strategy and starting to sell?" The result, he says, are declining numbers of publicly listed companies – fewer companies are choosing to make an IPO.

His solution is the LTSE.

"Modern companies measure progress over decades, not financial quarters. Investors who invest long term want to know not just how companies plan to produce value in the next quarter but for years to come. Employees, customers, suppliers, and communities count on companies to uphold their commitments and to do right by society."

In the LTSE, investors are taking a bet on the character of the founders. They believe that over time, like the Design Thinking squiggle, the messiness and the ambiguity will smooth out because you've got the right people solving a problem – with grit, patience and perseverance. It gives companies the space and time to keep figuring out how to do what they need to do before having to do a deal with the devil and list.

The LTSE asks: "Can you figure out what matters to your customers faster than what your competitors do?" It doesn't ask: "Can you make a short-term profit even if it means destroying long-term value. If you can't, we the shareholders will replace you with professional managers/execs who can."

It's interesting to me that Ries seems to have subsequently turned his attention away from Lean StartUp Co (working with corporates) to the LTSE. I wonder if he's seen enough of the corporate innovation movie to now choose to spend his time growing challengers to incumbents via the LTSE, rather than putting lipstick on pigs. I hope this isn't the case, because I've got to believe that our legacy organisations have the potential and energy to change. In South Africa, we don't have many other options.

Levels of work and the long-term leadership game

In organisational psychology terms, there's something called the Stratified Systems Theory. This organisational design theory indicates the level of work, or the level of complexity, that a person can effectively function at and the time delay between the work that you do and the impact it has on the customer. The following is a very simplistic way of describing these 'levels of work', but here goes...

The organisation experiences the impact of a call centre agent or customer-facing staffer within seconds. These people are custodians of transactions. The organisation sees the impact of a line manager's work within six months. These people are custodians of process. The organisation experiences the impact of a head of department's work within one to two years. These people are custodians of practice. The organisation experiences the impact of a functional head's work within three to four years. These people are custodians of goals. The organisation experiences the impact of a CEO's work after five years. This person is the custodian of strategy.

In this system, these modes of work relate to accountability and the capacity for each of these people – from the call centre staffer to the CEO – to affect strategy, see the big picture and drive organisational change.

In this structure, it would seem obvious that the higher your level of work and the greater the complexity and responsibility for managing the long-term fortunes of the business, the greater accountability you hold. And yet, our country has a culture, in both the public and private sectors, of reversing those polarities. The employees with the least influence and accountability suffer the greater consequences for any small mistake they may make, while those with the greatest accountability – the C-suiters, the CEO, ministers, presidents – seem to side-step any and all consequences for making trash decisions or making no decisions at all to safeguard the future of the company (or country) they've been tasked with steering. Not only do they seem to side-step consequences, but they get annual bonuses, for many consecutive years, long before evidence of the impact of their complex work can be validated.

I've started seeing short-termism and the executive and management incentives that support this behaviour in leaders – and even the shareholders and institutional investors that buy into this system – as part of the Grendel's Mom problem. Decisions are not driven by what's good for the business or the customer, but by what's good for the short-term oriented shareholders and short-term incentivised leaders. Wouldn't it be interesting to delay annual bonuses for line managers upwards, giving them a massive bonus only at the end of two, three, four or even five years, when evidence of the impact related to their level of work is verifiable?

If we're going to grow and nurture leaders who can hold space for innovation and agility, who take the long view, we cannot support them with short-term bonuses. Leaders incentivised by short-term bonuses won't drive any kind of innovation that creates systemic change. They're too invested in the status quo. And while they might incrementally improve the system, you can't move at that glacial pace and expect to keep up with competitors. Moreover, this form of broken mediocrity doesn't inspire change or trust, and certainly doesn't manage and utilise quality resources well.

Ultimately, culture as we understand it in organisations manifests in the leadership team. Similarly at a country level. We can't keep rewarding people with short-term bonuses and expecting the culture to change. If we really want to change the culture of status quo hires at the top, we have to change how they're incentivised. Wouldn't it be incredible if the business deferred bonuses until after the vision the CEO talked big about was realised? Their job is to realise vision. That's why they're the CEO after all.

What kind of quality leaders would we get if there was a correlation between level of work, the grit in achieving a vision for the long-term health of the organisation, and incentives? What kind of organisational change would we see?

Chicken or Pig

There's a ThinkWrong drill that I love using with my clients. It's an easy way for teams to sort themselves into lead and support roles. The concept is simple. After the work has been outlined, team members volunteer themselves into two roles for implementation: as chicken or pig.

A chicken forms part of the support team, contributing a healthy portion of its energy but not committing fully; the pig contributes it all, making the biggest sacrifice of the lot and taking accountability as team lead. It's a fun, brash analogy that works for moving processes along and inspiring action, but it's also a fantastically simplified version of levels of work in the Stratified Systems Theory. In this analogy, when an executive leader signs up, they're signing up to be the pig. They're not asked, "Are you going to be an ultimate flame carrier?", but "Are you going to be an ultimate flame carrier for 5 or 10 years?" Because the level that you're working at requires you to see it through. In fact, Stratified Systems Theory puts a horizon of 5 to 7 years for a CEO or GM of a large corporation, 7 to 10 for a Group CEO operating businesses in multiple territories.

This is all about grit. Patience, time, perseverance, delayed gratification. Grit. Everyone will say that embedding new ways of working is about organisational change, but for me, it's really about change at the top. The CEO, the C-suiters, the leadership team are the ultimate flame carriers for, and door keepers to, meaningful change and the means by which the organisation sets its culture.

When it comes to innovation, organisational perseverance and forward movement on innovation processes and projects, the leaders are the ones holding the keys in the ignition; they're the ones with the foot on the gas. If you as a leader choose to switch off the machine or slam on the brakes because your or the leadership team (and therefore the organisational culture) lacks grit – lacks perseverance and patience, and doesn't trust the time needed to start seeing results – no matter what process you start undertaking will eventually be crushed under the weight of tradition and old ways of working. There's a reason Christensen singled out managers as those who manage the status quo and ultimately lead the business with all the best intentions into irrelevancy.

Grit is a vital character trait for the leader and leadership team looking to empower the organisation with a strong innovation ecosystem. It is so fundamental to successful long-term corporate innovation that when I started writing this book, I was of the opinion that grit as a character trait valuable to innovation was disproportionately important relative to the others. Now, however, I see it a bit like the Marvel Cinematic Universe: every character (trait) has its role to play; they're all linked and you need all the pieces to come together in main or supporting parts for the whole to work optimally. For example, intellectual humility is needed for a growth mindset, and if your purpose isn't cognisant of the other, or contributing meaningfully in a positive way to the collective, it's possible that your grit could do more harm than good. Which brings me to other-centredness.

3. Other-centredness

How not being a jerk benefits innovation

"Our culture is a tough culture... it is a very, very aggressive culture." These are the words of Jeff Skilling, the disgraced former CEO of Enron, speaking in the company's heyday. It's from a tiny clip tucked into the 2005 documentary, *Enron: The Smartest Guys in the Room*, which was based on the eponymous bestseller by Bethany McLean and Peter Elkind. The two were *Fortune* magazine reporters at the time and McLean was one of the first journalists to ask the big question everyone else was too scared or wilfully ignorant to ask: What was Enron really worth?

 It might seem heavy-handed to pull Enron out as a poster child for corporate corruption after all these years, especially when there have been so many corporate scandals and implosions since then – Maddoff, the Lehmann Brothers and the subprime collapse, our very own Marcus Jooste and Steinhof, to name a few – but there's something so neat about this example for this chapter I couldn't let it slip by. You see, the Enron collapse was a direct result of a rotten ecosystem in general and a rotten top leadership in particular. Skilling himself is a poster child for predatory, individualistic leadership and how this trickles down and affects the business as a whole. He is the opposite of being purpose-driven for the collective; one of those psycho CEOs that Kiel talks about.

As a case in point, his favourite book is said to have been *The Selfish Gene* by Richard Dawkins, and the story goes that he used its premise to support his beliefs that people are inherently selfish and motivated by greed and fear.

"Jeff had a very Darwinian view of how the world worked", says McLean in the documentary. "He was famous for saying once, in Enron's early years, that money was the only thing that motivated people."

It was this dog-eat-dog view of the world that led Skilling to implement a management system that promoted intense internal competition and, presumably, supported his ever-riskier, ever more ruthless deceptions and schemes – hair-brained ideas that had the self-same *Forbes* naming Enron the Most Innovative Company six years in a row. The toxic effect of his character and leadership style is the basis of research papers and the cautionary tale of organisational culture specialists.

Things have changed somewhat since then. For one thing, we have a more realistic idea of how that sort of business ends. One could also argue that it's because of companies such as Enron that we're trying to build better, more humane business practices today. In fact, the 20th annual PwC *CEO Report* reminds us that the survey didn't start questioning CEOs about trust until 2002, "when the business community was reeling from accounting fraud scandals, the bursting of the dotcom bubble and the collapse of the equity markets". It's the 'dirty hands' problem I spoke about earlier.

"Since then, the financial crisis has catapulted trust into the limelight, and the after-effects of stagnant economic growth and spiralling debt levels continue to fuel a climate of mistrust."

If nothing else, for those who are trying to be better, to do differently, we have a good model of how not to be. And at least we have a more expanded understanding of what 'innovative' means now.

This is the least we should come away with, because, of course, there is still rot at the top; there are still leaders who shape business practice and culture to follow the idea that self-serving individualism trumps the collective good. After all, isn't that what got them to the top? Being the biggest, meanest bad-ass in town, where the only person to look out for was yourself, was, and in many cases remains, a powerful theme in the gladiatorial area of business. There are still those who have adopted, consciously or unconsciously, the belief that 'survival of the fittest' is the natural way of things and are therefore supportive of this behaviour.

But, as it turns out, interpreting 'survival of the fittest as strong versus weak' is misunderstanding Darwin's original meaning. He didn't even coin the term. That honour belongs to Herbert Spenser. Darwin himself argued that the social instinct for sympathy and 'social feeling' would harness greater rewards for the species. In his *Descent of Man*, he writes: "For those communities, which included the greatest number of the most sympathetic members, would flourish best, and rear the greatest number of offspring."

This feels remarkably apt for me even today, given an experience I was recently party of. Deep in the veld of the Greater Kruger National Park, six of us joined two armed guides for an immersive four-day survival trail. It was hard; a find-your-own-water, eat-what-you-catch kind of trail that put my soft city boy self through a serious test of endurance. Before we set off into the wild, our guides explained to us how the bush ecosystem epitomises *ubuntu*, the Zulu philosophy of: 'I am, because we are.' He introduced us to the seven laws of the bush, of which the final one, Rule 7, struck a particular chord for me. It was simply: 'Be kind.'

In 2020, evolutionary anthropologist Brian Hare and researcher Vanessa Woods published their cowritten work, *Survival of the Friendliest*. Their theory is that it wasn't homo sapiens' capacity to be bigger and better that made it a successful species, nor was it our big brains or technology. According to Hare and Woods, we existed with at least four other human species in the last 100,000 years, the most commonly known of which were the Neanderthals. They existed alongside us and had brains at least as big as ours. They were certainly stronger than us, and even had their own culture and tools.

"What made us evolutionarily fit was a remarkable kind of friendliness, a virtuosic ability to coordinate and communicate with others that allowed us to achieve all the cultural and technical marvels in human history."

This fits with what we know about the brain now – that we're hardwired for altruism. Numerous studies conducted into the neurobiology of the brain have revealed that humans get off on being generous. Known as the 'helper's high', it's a feeling that doesn't diminish over time in the way that the pleasure of receiving does (referred to as hedonic adaptation). The altruism instinct is hardwired in humans for social interaction and support, cooperation and social cohesion. It's not that we're all 100% Care Bear, but that we're as naturally inclined to think of others and the collective good as we are to think of only ourselves and our personal gain.

"What people don't understand is that it's actually very costly to be the Alpha male", said Woods in a BBC interview. "It can be incredibly stressful [since] you're always looking over your shoulder. [The notion of the] survival of the fittest as it's being interpreted to be the Alpha male will make you the most successful is not actually how it goes; it doesn't go that way in nature and it doesn't go that way in the corporate environment."

This idea of contribution to the well-being of others is something increasingly referred to as 'other-centredness' – the capacity to think about and act for people other than yourself. Much of our Western business practices to date – from company or product inception to marketing and consuming – has riffed off self-centredness, the idea that the individual need or desire is above all.

But thanks to the fall-out from self-serving psycho CEOs like Skilling and the growing awareness of climate change and resource abuse, the concept of other-centredness is slowly starting to creep into business literature. Sure, you're more likely hear the 'soft skills' words that circle around other-centredness, such as kindness, generosity, compassion and trust, but I like to think of other-centredness as an umbrella phrase for all of these; a sort of much more acceptable hold-all phrase for 'not being a jerk'.

Duckworth makes the trait of other-centredness an integral component of her theory of purpose motivating grit. But I believe there's something to say about it as a standalone character trait and how it influences a leader's success, especially when driving any form of innovation project underway within the company.

Purpose is what the world needs you to do; it helps to solve a hairy, scary problem that will take multiple generations to solve. Other-centredness, on the other hand, is what a person or people in your world need you to do, and that can be done, here and now, today. If you embrace it often enough, it will change the world long-term. It's like sowing light seeds. It's being kind. It's Rule 7.

Other-centredness is a long-term strategy

Don't expect other-centredness to be listed under traditional leadership styles. In workaday reality it takes time and effort, it feels inconvenient, it's energy-intensive. It is the diagrammatic opposite of a short-term attitude.

Let me explain.

There's a micro and macro view on the positive effects of other-centredness here. In your day-to-day dealings with your peers and employees, it's a trait that will benefit your relationships by building trust, a key ingredient to effective long-term innovation. This is largely what I'll be focusing on in this chapter, but as I do, I want to contain the message in the broader view of how other-centredness is necessary for long-term thinking and supports long-term success.

What I love about people like Katlego and his cofounders at Yoco is that they've gone about solving a juicy problem for themselves that is genuinely a problem for other people. Their's is a solid example of other-centredness, human-centred design and radical problem-solving at work. But the value of their work extends beyond even that because what they're doing doesn't uplift just one user at a time – it uplifts entire communities and builds on the country's economy in real terms and at the grassroots level; it's a feedback loop that works for everyone. A healthier economy means better business for them, the better business they can offer, the better the business of the entrepreneurs they serve. This is the true face of effective innovation.

From a leadership perspective, the 21st century isn't only about solving problems for other people or specific groups of people – even if they're problems that you might care deeply about – but solving them in a way that serves future generations and society at large.

What's been interesting for me to see is how this is expressing itself in small and meaningful ways in problem-solving practices on the ground.

When we launched Minivations at FNB, innovation was no longer the domain of sexy, big-budgeted product people and teams where very often big egos found happy homes to grow even bigger. Minivations enabled people who were humble custodians (or victims!) of processes and policies to come out of the woodwork as innovators and make small but meaningful changes that were kind to both the external customer and their colleagues – the internal customer. They took friction and frustration out, or lowered the levels of pain, at least. They didn't have to do this. Sure, they could win a few eBucks, but certainly not enough to change their lives or the trajectory of their careers or show them into the limelight. Minivators, in my experience, were kind.

What differentiates 21st century leadership from 20th century leadership is embedded in this other-centredness and longer-term mindset. We have too much data now to pretend that short-term thinking is viable going forward. We can no longer support the leaders who think and act like Skilling, Steinhoff and their ilk. It's not good for people and our communities, and it's certainly not good for the business in the long run.

Trust me, this is totally going to hurt a bit

I was recently involved in a long-term process with a company that was looking to prototype a challenger operating model as a way to embed new ways of working. It was an eight-month deep dive (yup, not all prototypes can progress at the speed of products!) that involved employees from all tiers and areas of the business and aimed to introduce the concepts of human-centred design and Agile and Lean and so on to the staff and embed these into their work systems.

At the end of each phase, before the next iteration of the operating model prototype was to be pitched to the leadership team, we would compile a sort of wish-list of what the team would want to ask of them. The line-up of usual suspects was always the same: time, money, a demarcated space to work in... but there was also a consistent call for leadership honesty around the programme and requests for leadership to confirm their commitment and buy-in to the process. The overwhelming response from the teams was always: we're loving this, we're learning, we're feeling valued and committed, we feel motivated and like we're contributing meaningfully – please don't turn this into an experimental exercise that goes nowhere. The common refrain was: "We don't want another small oasis of meaning in the desert of business-as-usual."

What struck me about this was that, even though the team was in the middle of a change moment in the organisation's history, even though leadership was involved and hands-on in the process, the people on the ground still didn't believe it was really going to change anything. "We've been here before and nothing changes", was a regular plaintive cry.

Without trust in the leadership team driving the prototyping, without trust that something was really going to come of their hard work, what would motivate them to keep bringing their best work?

Trust in leadership and management teams and how this affects employee engagement and productivity is a relatively new area of study. It's being seen as a component of 'social capital', itself a newish arena. In 2017, a Harvard Law paper, *The Role of Social Capital in Corporations*, defined social capital as "the quality of the relationships that a firm, and its executives and employees, have built with other stakeholders" and placed it alongside physical capital, human capital and intellectual capital in corporations.

These are great steps in the right direction and I'm glad to see that the value of this trust between leadership and employees is a topic that's finally starting to take its first tentative steps outside of the domain of the HR researchers and execs. And it has to, because by affecting engagement and productivity, it affects the company's bottom line.

In 2017, The Engagement Institute (a massive collaboration of The Conference Board, Sirota-Mercer, Deloitte, ROI, The Culture Works and Consulting LLP) released a study of 1,500 respondents revealing that disengaged employees cost companies between US$450 and 550 billion a year. That's not small change. The study, *DNA of Engagement: How Organizations Can Foster Employee Ownership of Engagement*, looked specifically at team dynamics and found that compelling missions (there's that purpose-driven grit we were talking about) and highly trusted relationships were two vital elements to helping employees take more responsibility for their own engagement.

Two particular insights into driving a culture of engagement stood out for me: "Teams can't function without trust and integrity... team leaders cannot be effective, engaging leaders if they don't establish trust, act with integrity, and empower their teams." And: "Highly engaged teams can help organisations innovate."

Again, anyone in innovation circles will recognise this as obvious.

We've already touched on this. Innovation needs trust. Each person, each team, needs to be able to trust that collaboration across work levels is possible and respected. They need to trust that free thinking is allowed without blowback. They must trust that the freedom to fail and to learn from that failure won't incur consequences to their career. They need the trust to speak up and raise their hand, even if that means speaking up to point out flaws in the system or raising their hands to work on projects their line managers are against. Teams need to trust that funding and resources won't be yanked before processes are figured out.

Leaders also need to learn how to trust. They need to trust that budgets and time will be put to good use, and that the output will justify the input of these resources. In my experience, there can be some particular hurdles to overcome here, especially with legacy organisations that are not fully committed to innovation and innovative thinking as a necessary toolset for the future. For example, Company A doesn't really want to embrace new ways of working even though markets are demanding change, so they start some kind of process to ease their worries, but instead of sending their brightest and best to the table, they send their difficult employees, those with poor performance, attendance and disciplinary records. It's an easy way to get rid of these guys in a unionised environment and under the constraints of an employee-friendly Labour Relations Act. This is particularly problematic when you're trying to tout the innovation-friendly principle 'it's okay to fail'. Faced with slackers and big egos who ignore human-centred design, you've got a recipe for disaster.

Trust, therefore, is very much a two-way street. Eric Reis talks about trust a lot in *The Leader's Guide*. It was his follow-up to *The Lean Startup* and is a collection and distillation of his very practical, very results-oriented process that he uses with executives and leaders at both early-stage start-ups and massive blue-chip corporations. (It's a worthwhile read if you want to know more about the process and how to implement it in your organisation.) In *The Leader's Guide*, Reis talks about internal entrepreneurs, or intrapreneurs, and as a leader how you might be able to best maximise their skills. What it boils down to is simple: "At the heart of entrepreneurial management", he says, "is a shared trust between leaders and entrepreneurs."

So how do you go about building this trust with your team?

Building trust – one step at a time

Mark Murphy is the founder of Leadership IQ and leads one of the world's largest studies on goal setting and leadership. In one of his surveys, *How To Build Trust In The Workplace*, he questioned more than 7,000 people – from executives to managers and employees – on why people do or don't trust their leaders. "The first thing we discovered was that approximately 32% of a worker's loyalty is the result of feeling trust towards their boss."

Trust is different things to different people. Some say it's a firm belief in the reliability, truth and ability of someone or something. Others that it's the firm belief that someone has your best interests at heart. Either way, we can all agree that it's fragile. How to foster and maintain it is a variable and seemingly subjective list depending on who you're speaking to and which study you're reading.

At the start of this book, I mentioned Fred Kiel's *Return on Character* and the four principles he believes goes into constructing a good leader, namely: integrity, compassion, responsibility and forgiveness. Then there's Dovey's Mandela list: identify stakeholders and reach consensus on the core, respect, honour commitments, forgive and reconcile and so on. Back in South Africa, the *Leadership, Character and its Development* study by De Braine and Verrier revealed a wide array of varying beliefs people hold around what builds trust, including in one instance 'competence, connection and character' and 'integrity/faithfulness' in another.

However, it's interesting to me that when it comes to trust in the realm of business relationships, it's not considered obvious to turn to the relationship experts in this matter. After all, your work colleagues, peers and employees are the people you're spending most of your day with, and every interaction between you and them feeds into the loop that is the relationship you share with them, no matter how superficial.

So for this section on how to actually go about inspiring trust, I've turned to the work of Drs John and Julie Gottman, founders of The Gottman Institute and award-winning researchers and clinical psychologists in the field of relationships for almost 40 years. Dr John Gottman is also the author of, among other books, *The Science of Trust*, and has done a ton of work in the trust metric as it relates specifically to intimate relationships.

"If my numbers are right", he says, "it's smart to take the risk of trusting people, and it is also smart to know whom not to trust".

He suggests five criteria for evaluating the trustworthiness of others, namely honesty, transparency, accountability, ethics and alliance. These ring true for me from my experience of relationships in the work environment, inside and out of the innovation bubble, and I believe these are a great foundation for seeing how others will learn to trust you as their leader – or not.

1.   Honesty

I saw a great interview with Rita Gunther McGrath at a CNBC @Work summit on a panel that focused on the value of building trust within the workplace. McGrath is a strategic management scholar and professor of management at the Columbia Business School who's known for her work on strategy, innovation and entrepreneurship. She's also authored a number of books on the topic and has written about the distrust that's developed from the short-termist nature of public companies emphasising profits over people.

In the panel, which she sat on with HR industry heavyweights Francine Katsoudas of Cisco and Jayne Parker of The Walt Disney Company, she said about communicating with trust: "If you're the kind of leader who says 'don't bring me bad news and don't bring me problems if you don't also have a solution', guess what? You're not going to get brought bad news and you're not going to get problems, and so you are going to be left with a humongous giant blind spot. So part of the lack of trust is if I don't trust that I can speak up and that I'm in a psychologically safe space, I'm not going to tell you what you probably need most to hear."

Clear, honest and open communication is imperative for co-creating a workplace based on trust and mutual respect. Without it you lose vital information and underplay your assets. This is particularly true if you're in a process of prototyping new systems and ways of working. Your team needs to feel safe to call out weak spots in a plan or say it failed.

Trust cannot be built in an environment of deceit, obfuscation or stonewalling; if this is how you communicate with your team, you're not going to get results.

2. Transparency

Transparency is closely linked to honesty for obvious reasons. But aiming to be honest doesn't have the scope that transparency does. You can be honest about your personal shortcomings and failures to illustrate grit and build a sense of camaraderie with your team, but that doesn't automatically imply that you'll be forthcoming about employee data tracking or leadership team-building outcomes.

Although it can change from company to company, transparency is generally about playing open books with your employees, your stakeholders and the public. It can sound crazy to do so, but in the current world of tech and data availability, it seems futile to remain stuck in a mindset of what happens behind the closed doors of the C-suiters' offices will stay behind closed doors. We just know that isn't true anymore.

In the 20th PwC *CEO Survey*, which deals particularly with trust and transparency, Bob Moritz, the global chairman of PwC, writes that globalisation and technology have jointly enabled a massive increase in trade and financial flows and global online traffic, forcing society to think about how information is accessed and consumed. The result, he says, is that transparency has become a key consideration of how business leaders engage with stakeholders – from consumers to employees.

Of course, transparency is a balancing act. You can't share everything with your customers and employees, but opacity doesn't foster the trust needed for good creative thinking.

That team I was talking about earlier that didn't trust that what they were doing was a real systems change were facing transparency issues. They didn't believe that the leadership team was really allowing the process to unfold and become reality because they hadn't been let in on the bigger picture. The big guys at the top hadn't been transparent about their long-term plans or their motivations. And with good reason. Their sense was that they didn't want to worry stakeholders or cause ructions in the wider employee base. But the consequences were clear in the team output.

You have to know how to manage transparency to your benefit. Don't hide relevant information when sharing it could build trust in you and confidence in your leadership. Protectionism as a leadership attitude is a tough habit to break, but failure to do so only breeds a culture of suspicion, rumours and distrust. Employees will smell the dwang no matter how much you try to hide it.

There's another aspect to transparency that I like. Better tech means easier access to and greater transparency around information regarding products, companies and their employees. This means, if you'd like your business to succeed long-term, you have a stronger need for greater accountability and ethical practices.

"Increased transparency", says Moritz, "demands a new way of communicating, a higher level of accountability, an elevated approach to leadership, and indeed, a deeper focus on trust, purpose and the inherent human connection that has brought us closer together".

3.   Ethical actions

Moritz points out that as tech and public awareness starts creating – and sometimes forcing – transparency, execs need to become more conscious of and fully grasp the ethical implications of their decisions and actions, "developing the moral muscle to make the right decisions and stand behind them".

Moreover, he says, our new workforce is hyper aware of purpose, demanding not just the 'how' but the 'why'. "Enduring winners will be leaders who develop a two-way relationship – whether with customers, employees, or society at large – based on reliability and ethical behaviour." Gottman refers to this as 'walk the talk' and it's a message that's consistent in business literature. You can't expect honesty if you don't speak and act with honesty. You can't expect employees to be curious and motivated if you're never asking questions and knock off every Friday at noon. Acting consistently with the principles, values and beliefs you expect your teams to adhere to, leads to confidence in your management message.

There is something else I'd like to add under 'ethical actions' and that is demonstrating expertise and good judgment; showcasing your expertise with clarity and confidence. You can't fake it 'til you make it. Employees are more likely to trust you as a leader if they believe you know what you're talking about and have the experience and discernment to make good decisions. I was listening to Ray Dalio's book *Principles* recently. He makes a comment that great people worth hiring have both strong character and competence. He goes on to say if they only have either one of these – not both – don't hire them. It speaks to De Braine and Verrier's "competence, connection and character". It makes me wonder if they are equally weighted.

4.   Accountability

Keep your promises and follow through on your commitments. Simple. This is the first level of building trust through accountability. Do what you say you're going to do. But accountability expands beyond this. It's about taking responsibility for your own actions and failures. Admitting when you get it wrong makes you human and relatable, but it also encourages and fosters honesty.

This capacity to tell, not hide, the truth is difficult. Accountability takes courage and integrity. It is not a trait for those of weak character. If you're leading a team in an innovation project, whether it's a product or a new way of working, there can be no passing the hot potato when something breaks or plans don't work out. Accountability as a leader speaks to me also of gratitude and appreciation for what you've been given: the chance to lead. And this comes with the responsibility of providing air cover and taking bullets when your team is under attack. It's a weird blessing in disguise kind of perspective, but it's there.

5.   Proof of alliance

Almost everyone I know in the service industry has a story about the one boss who once backed them up in a tight spot. Have you ever wondered why this becomes an anecdote worth sharing? Or why it's usually only one historical moment, so unique in its appearance it's worth remembering? Proof of alliance is the diagrammatic opposite of CYA – cover your arse. It means that you show your team that you have their back. That they're not expected to operate as defensive solo artists, but that they're supported and led in a team; that you won't throw them the hot potato that belongs to you when things get heated. As a facilitator in this arena for many years, I usually coach my innovation leaders along the following lines...

Good communication is about being an effective listener. It means you respect them enough to listen to them; you are invested in them and their input. In feedback on that leadership IQ survey, Murphy says: "We discovered that the number one driver of whether an employee will trust their boss is the extent to which employees felt that their boss responded constructively when they shared their work problems.

"Having a boss who listens constructively to a worker's on-the-job problems was found to be the strongest predictor of loyalty to an organisation, accounting for fully 26% of their wanting to stay or go."

'Kindness' might not be a word that rolls off your tongue easily, but it will be felt in how you engage your actions or speech intended to help others. Learn to communicate effectively, listen constructively and ask meaningful questions ('What's getting in your way?', 'What's frustrating you?', 'Do you see a way around this?', 'How can I help you?'). If you need to get a coach to do so, then do it.

Demonstrate confidence in them. Don't lecture and direct. Nothing will kill the innovative spirit and silence collective wisdom quicker than being a HIPPO who demands attention and that their ideas be elevated. Doing so only implies that you don't trust the value of their input or decision-making abilities. No good innovative ideas will flourish in that environment.

As a leader who hopes to build innovative thinking into your team, your job is to provide guidance, structure and air cover; it's to actively create the kind of environment that inspires collaboration and an exchange of dialogue and ideas. Again, you've got to have the kind of character that will be able to step back and listen, encourage and support; that understands it's not about you.

Have their back. Do you have their best interests at heart instead of acting only out of self-interest? This is more than just supporting them and listening to them when the shit hits the fan. This is about supporting your employees by supporting their growth. When you invest in your people through training or development, upskilling or reskilling programmes, you demonstrate that you're invested in them and their future. By taking the proactive initiative to be helpful, you build trust and promote engagement.

It's not as easy as it looks

When you start your innovation journey, no matter how it looks, it's going to blow all pretence out the window. Trust is not something that can be faked.

As a leader of any capacity, especially in a big, corporate environment, building that trust is a process in itself. Trust is tenuous. Building trust can be easy if you're authentic and take responsibility, but it can be difficult and inconvenient if you struggle to connect to people. If you need to work on it, you will need to work. This is not something that can be left to the HR department – not if you want to build a legacy of being a worthy leader regardless of which organisation you find yourself in. 21st century leaders need self-awareness about their own character strengths and struggles to model the behaviour for their team and assess individual employees on these.

Although what builds trust varies from researcher to researcher and organisation to organisation, one thing is similar across the board: be consistent. As you read through these though, don't worry if you find yourself 'falling short' of the suggested mark. The capacity to build trust in others is not an inherent skill we all have. Instead, it's a set of behaviours that you can foster and build on, strengthen and get progressively good at. We can practice getting better at anything, including how to build trust.

This isn't going to happen overnight, but you can build it very practically into your innovation process. For example, part of the incremental funding model for data-driven, innovation experiments is about building trust in small steps. The people in this work need to trust the people who have asked them to do this work, and vice versa. If you've got the right people in the mix, you've got to trust them and give them the space to tackle this work. But equally they have to generate the empirical evidence that they're on track, even if they're on track in a messy way.

That's the way to build trust when it comes to relationships – in small increments.

The servant leader

When Wade van Niekerk's foot hit the 400m finish line at the Rio Games in 2016, breaking Michael Johnson's 17-year record by an astonishing 0.15 seconds, a 74-year-old woman in the stands won her first Olympic gold.

Anna 'Tannie Ans' Botha, a seasoned coach from Namibia, was Van Niekerk's unlikely Olympic trainer. He approached her for training in late 2012 at the University of the Free State, where she'd been head coach of track and field coach since 1990. The story goes that she was so unlike the stereotype of any trainer that it took a full hour for her to convince security to let her gain access to him after he'd won.

When I first heard about Tannie Ans, there was something about her and Van Niekerk's story that struck a chord for me. I was moved that behind this record-breaking athlete, this world star, was an unassuming, steadfast, talented and supportive leader in her field, guiding him to ultimate victory. But I couldn't quite put my finger on what the definitive term was that she reminded me of. It was only a few years later when I read one of the many articles subsequently written about her.

Following her award for Coaching Achievement at the IAAF Athletics Awards in Monaco in 2017, Tannie Ans was interviewed for a feature by the World Athletics Organisation. The article opens with the following quote from her:

"Life", says Anna Botha, "isn't about the years you're living; it's about what you contributed in those years to your fellow human beings".

And there it was. Servant leadership.

That's what Tannie Ans did. The kind of leadership that not only enables, but when there's success doesn't try to grab the limelight (to be fair, it came looking for her!). Servant leaders are those who give other people opportunities; who serve people when they see something in them that they can't see in themselves. Who take some personal risk by providing an opportunity for them.

In my work with legacy corporations, I see these servant leaders when they engage their people in our workshops and involve their teams in grassroots problem-solving. It's a beautiful thing to watch and be part of, especially in the typically inflexible and hierarchical set-up of the corporate giant.

Between the old guard and the new

'Servant leadership' was defined in 1970 by Robert K Greenleaf in his essay *The Servant as Leader*. The concept is simple enough: "Leaders whom we trust and want to follow achieve moral authority by being servants to followers and organisations, not by wielding titles or using coercive power."

Greenleaf went on to further develop the philosophy of the servant leader, starting up the Greenleaf Centre for Servant Leadership and kicking off what would become a new area of study in leadership. By 1998, 'servant leadership' had become a topic of research and by 2015, social scientists were developing and validating instruments and describing servant leadership in peer-reviewed literature.

Much like the subject of trust, it's a wide, historically interpretive field where every author and researcher has put their own spin on different dimensions of servant leadership according to their research. I've settled on the outcome of the 2019 paper by Nathan Eva et al. called *Servant Leadership: A systematic review and call for future research*.

In this exposition, which was based on all the work to date on the topic, they offer a new definition of servant leadership as an "other-oriented approach to leadership, manifested through one-on-one prioritising of follower individual needs and interests, and outward reorienting of their concern for self towards concern for others within the organisation and the larger community".

In other words: other-centredness.

As you can imagine, it's not like this has been the go-to leadership style of the global corporate arena until now.

Who are we serving?

To simplify the illustration with a binary, you could see servant leadership as the diagrammatic opposite of traditional leadership.

On the one side, traditional leaders use power and control to drive performance; they see employees as resources, success as short-term outputs and wins, and customers as challenges to overcome. It's a top-down approach that tells people what to do and stresses the importance and value of the 'higher ups' as opposed to the 'resources'. It serves the individual in power.

On the other side, servant leadership sees leadership as an opportunity to serve others. It's a bottom-up approach that shares power and control, that collaborates and listens, to drive engagement with employees. It aims to build and support its people, work with customers as allies, and aims for organisational longevity. It is the ultimate human-centred design leadership. I see 'authentic leadership' as falling within its realm. It serves the collective first, meeting the needs of people before reaping the rewards for themselves. This doesn't mean we have to get Disney about it. This isn't some kind of ultimate sacrifice. The kind of person who will be drawn to the idea of servant leadership will get a kick out of doing so; they'll view legacy as important and will thrive off positive feedback from this.

It reminds me a bit of Rassie Erasmus in *Chasing the Sun*, a documentary following the spectacular 2019 South African Rugby World Cup win. Just in case you don't know, Rassie was the Springbok coach who took the team from zeroes to heroes in just 18 months, from a messy two seasons under the former coach. I found it interesting that Rassie talks about 'win first'. It's an example of a leader encouraging his players to be other-centred and their goal customer-centric – giving the Springboks' customers (the sports-mad SA public) what they need: a reminder of what it feels like to win! Then scratch your own itches. He also structured things around what the players needed. Psychological safety associated with contracts, selections and so on. But he doesn't just demonstrate other-centredness... he asks them to do the same. A kind of 'Other-centredness 2.0'. As a leader, do it yourself, but then insist that your team do it too – or encourage them to find another team.

Whatever your personal motives, how you go about engineering an organisation culture – through power and control, or other-centredness – is going to have organisational impact. And you simply cannot create a culture of trust with ego-based, self-centred character traits that favour a power and dominance position. Not in the long term. This way lies distrust, rebellion, passivity and a lack of creativity and engagement.

But what does it matter?

Let's say you're leading a team on an innovation project. It's your job, as the leader, not to dominate and control outcomes, but to guide and support. You are, or are part of, the air cover that helps your team go about the business of figuring out the solution. In this situation, without an element of servant leadership, the fundamentals of good innovation fall down.

Those attempting to lead from a position of power control aren't going to make space for collaboration; they won't be able to provide a platform for the collective wisdom of their people or take a step back to let others shine. They're not going to accept that they may not have the answer to everything and that someone three levels down from their pay grade may have a meaningful solution. They're not going to accept failure or take calculated risks because the blow-back might affect their short-term plans. They're not going to work for the long-term health of the company because once they leave what does it matter... and so on.

The ripple effect of being or becoming a servant leader builds organisational strength from the inside out by building on the relationships you're able to foster with your employees.

The other day I heard a story from a friend of mine who works as People Ops for a growth start-up. It was the end of 2020 and the performance-based bonuses were obviously – given the mess of the year – not going to pay out because no one had been able to meet their targets. The CEO, however, had met most of his targets and was therefore in line to get a pay-out. His solution? Split the money five ways between his top management team. Her response was gushing.

"The trust and commitment I now feel towards him has just ballooned", she told me. "I mean, it was already pretty much complete, but honestly, it's double now."

It wasn't the first time I'd heard about this sort of thing happening. Over the first COVID wave that rocked businesses, the managers of a major retailer I was working closely with opted for pay-raise stalls so that they could keep paying their people salaries over lockdown. They made sure their employees were looked after and felt secure. When a debrief was done a few months later, the feedback from the ground was resounding: we feel trusted, we feel appreciated, we feel safe.

Interestingly, the rapid change in circumstances also meant that new ways of working prototypes that were in the pipeline for this particular retailer had to be fast-tracked. It meant that, whether management or leadership were ready or not, they had to jump in and provide the support for staff on the ground to fill in the gaps where they were happening; they had to hand over some control, do away with laborious processes, and listen to what employees on the ground were telling them about customer engagement. The emergency made it impossible for leadership to second guess every step of every new roll-out. They had to trust their frontline staff with more autonomy to make snap decisions, work across divisions and take on more responsibility. The feedback was right on track: we're motivated, we want more, we feel trusted and we believe we're part of something.

It's unfortunate that many leaders of legacy organisations need this kind of crisis to let go. That they need to be backed into an emergency situation before they realise they need to change and get agile.

When we try to quantify the value of adopting servant leadership and all its attendant markers: other-centredness, intellectual humility, purpose, trust, the bigger picture... we have to look deeper than the immediate ROI in dollar signs that we think it should represent.

The effects of adopting this stance will eventually lead to $$, but through the channels of employee retention, reduced absenteeism, employee engagement, talent attraction and the resulting increased profitability from these actions, as well as increased customer experience due to improved employee experiences. Happy employees, breed happy customers.

It takes a whole lot of courage

This isn't about being a people-pleaser or a push-over.

"This orientation towards others reflects the leader's resolve, conviction, or belief that leading others means a movement away from self-orientation. This is in stark contrast to other leadership approaches that focus on the advancement of the leaders' ambition or agenda", says Eva and co in *Servant Leadership*.

"Their resolve to serve others emanates out of their self-concept as an altruist, moral person. It therefore follows that servant leadership is not about being courteous or friendly. By default, it requires a strong sense of self, character, and psychological maturity."

No one is expecting miracles here. It would be naive to believe that every business, at all levels, would find it easy to shift gear from one form of leadership to another.

To be honest, I'm not sure how many people in positions of power would willingly opt to do the character work. Those 'psychopath CEOs' and power-drunk line managers don't really like these new ways of working, where their customers – both internal and external – genuinely get served before they do, where their colleagues and communities also win. How could they if their prime directive is themselves and getting that bonus paid? Even more so, if they get a kick from holding and exerting power, or boosting their sense of self-worth based on holding a title/senior position. Like Eva and his fellow writers say: "Those who are unwilling to serve others are unfit to be a servant leader."

But for anyone not actively trying to be a jerk – and I'm going to make an assumption here based on the fact that you're reading this, that you're not going out of your way to be one – it's worth trying to be better. Even if you're totally up for the ride, it doesn't mean it's going to come to you easily. Our traditional set up favours the Jeff Skillings of the world. And, frankly, every one of us in corporate probably has a bit of Skilling in us. One of my grandpas was an iconoclast reverend within the Anglican church. His mission was to democratise faith by making it more accessible to everyday people by removing all the pomp, ceremony, and high falutin' language from church services. I remember him telling me that the biggest test of a person's character comes when they are presented with a big injection of money or power. My character has certainly been challenged by both.

If being a servant leader doesn't come naturally, becoming a servant leader – and I believe all leaders have the capacity to become one – is an act of will. It will require remaining conscientious, always, about how you approach your power and control. It will require cultivating intentionality about investing time, energy and care into listening to and empowering your people. It will ask all of this and more from you, but it will also serve you, your people and the organisation in the long run.

Good relationships

One of the longest-running longitudinal studies ever done started in 1938 during the Great Depression with 268 Harvard sophomores.

The aim of the research, which formed part of *The Harvard Study of Adult Development*, was to reveal the clues to leading healthy and happy lives. In 1970, the study expanded to include 456 Boston inner-city residents – kids utterly unlike the Harvard guys. Over the almost 80 years that the study ran, tracking these people's lives, the scientists made a remarkable discovery.

It wasn't genes, upbringing, access to healthcare, wealth, fame or a 'good' neighbourhood that contributed to the overall well-being of the participants.... it was the state of their relationships.

"The surprising finding is that our relationships and how happy we are in our relationships has a powerful influence on our health", said Robert Waldinger, director of the study and professor of psychiatry at Harvard

Medical School. "Taking care of your body is important, but tending to your relationships is a form of self-care too. That, I think, is the revelation."

While the study's outcomes were heavily slanted towards personal relationships, and in particular intimate relationships, in his TED Talk on the study Waldinger lists the following as the first big lesson they learned from the study.

"Social connections are really good for us and loneliness kills", he says. "It turns out that people who are more socially connected to family, to friends, to community are happier, they're physically healthier and they live longer than people who are less well connected."

According to Waldinger, loneliness is pretty much toxic and makes health decline earlier in midlife, brain functioning decline sooner, and generally shortens life compared to those who don't consider themselves lonely.

It may seem disconnected to anything to do with work, but when 60–80% of your time is spent thinking and breathing business, who you surround yourself with – and how – is going to matter.

When I established the CLC meet-ups (the community of practice for local corporate innovation leaders I mentioned earlier), I did so because entrepreneurship and intrapreneurship can both be lonely places. You're on the outside, it's competitive, it's risky. The meetups were more that 'just' networking; it was a support group for leaders who were different thinkers and radical problem solvers. There's reason the saying 'It's lonely at the top' has stood the test of time.

Social intelligence for innovation

Ena Inesi is an Associate Professor of Organisational Behaviour at the London Business School and for more than a decade has focused her research on power and how it affects relationships and decision-making. Working with fellow researchers into the topic, Inesi has found that power can twist good relationships.

Significantly, power alters our beliefs about others' generosity and affects how we respond to those around us. Writing for the London Business School, she said: "The power-holders start to distance themselves from those they were once close to. Niggling thoughts seed in their minds. They start to question the motives of those around them: 'Do people like me because I'm me or because of my position? Are my jokes actually funny or are people just laughing because I'm the boss? Did that person do me a favour because they want something?'"

The result, she says, is that the power-holder is less likely to reciprocate if they believe the favours were selfishly motivated. "[Favours] make power-holders wary and impede the sort of friendly behaviour required for close relationships to develop and last."

Trust withers and commitment wanes as those personal connections dwindle.

It's not just interpersonal relationships that suffer, it's the relationship with self that suffers. Inesi says that their research has found that, far from being a personally liberating experience, power traps the power-holder in limiting self-identity. Being done a favour causes the power-holder to self-objectify, she says. "In other words, they internalise the view that they believe others hold of them: 'If someone thinks that I am valuable because of my power, then that must be what makes me valuable.'"

They see people as acting warmly towards them because of their influence, not because of who they are or because the favour-doer is of good character. Desiring to remain attractive and important to others, says Inesi, they then push to increase their power further or emphasise it with status goods. "It's little wonder then that those with power – to whatever degree or in whatever guise – may feel isolated."

Power comes at the cost of relationships. If your leadership motivation is self-centred, if your style is defensive and your purpose short-termist and self-serving, your relationships will suffer. And the antidote can only be servant leadership, other-centredness and its attendant components. The capacity to see beyond yourself and interact with your peers and employees with a sense of humanity, compassion, kindness...

If this doesn't appeal to you as a leader, it may be a good reminder that these are qualities needed to be a great innovator today. Without these qualities it's impossible to harness the impact of human-centred design in finding solutions for the 21st century problems that both your internal and external customers face.

Diversity can be a beautiful foundation for great relationships

The value of good relationships supporting innovation reminds me of Peter Thiel's reported approach to hiring practices. Thiel is the tech billionaire investor who cofounded PayPal and was one of Facebook's first outside investors. He's also the author of *Zero to One* and is known for his insights into start-ups, given his experience of investing in and working with them. Among some of his more controversial approaches, is his take on diversity within the start-up's initial founder bubble.

In a 2007 *Fortune* article titled, *The PayPal Mafia* (which says it all, really), Thiel and cofounder Max Levchin were interviewed about the rise and rise of PayPal and how it became a "petri dish for entrepreneurs" (its founding fathers include Elon Musk, Roelof Botha and David Sacks). And it all started with selection bias.

"They were looking for a specific type of candidate", writes *Fortune* senior editor Jeffrey M. O'Brien. "They wanted competitive, well-read, multilingual individuals who, above all else, had a proficiency in math... In other words they were looking for people like themselves."

Thiel recalls that they started by hiring people in their circles. "I hired friends from Stanford, and Max brought in people from the University of Illinois."

The commonality meant they were much more likely to get along, share a vision and enjoy the same life and work culture. "All of this is about self-selecting for people just like you", says Levchin. "He thinks like me, he's just as geeky, and he doesn't get laid very often. Great hire! We'll get along perfectly."

It's interesting to me that the success of start-up founders was (is) often premised on these shared values and lifestyles, creating a solid base for them to make a big impact. There's no fuel burned on trying to align with each other or understand and overcome communication and culture barriers.

When I first heard about their approach, it occurred to me that many of the start-up early success stories start out with mates just gunning for an idea. It made me wonder about corporates and whether the creativity boost you get from diversity – education, skillsets, sex, gender, race, background – can balance out the fuel you burn trying to get everyone aligned.

Then I realised that the need for commonality here wasn't about working on great innovations, but rather the need to be easily understood. Selection bias didn't stop the PayPal founders from falling out. It was a way, unconsciously, to force a culture of relationship and it worked for a while by selecting for superficial connections.

But this approach is only ever going to work in the short term. And there is something we can learn here.

Cofounder fall-out in start-ups is a documented problem. Academic and best-selling author Noam Wasserman details this in his book *The Founder's Dilemmas*, in which he outlines, as the title suggests, the main challenges start-up founders face, from questions on whether to go solo to who to hire, how to assign roles and how to manage investors and succession.

The book kicks off almost immediately with the matter of those pesky 'people problems', saying that 65% of 'high potential' start-ups fail as a result of co-founder conflict. The top issue? Internal niggles within the management team. In short: relationship troubles.

At the start of the venture, founder stability is high, says Wasserman, but over time he shows that it flags significantly, especially when founders were friends. The problem comes in with the assumptions we make about each other and how we deal with conflict. We assume that boundaries and parameters are understood. We avoid conflict to avoid hurting the relationship outside of the work environment.

This is not how good relationships are formed. Instead, we see this work being done in more diverse groups.

With acquaintances – say, colleagues from diverse areas – it's understood that relationships will need to be built. Work will need to be done to understand each other and to challenge biases, which means that assumptions are fewer and conflict expected and so mitigated for. Good communication becomes something that is consciously improved on, instead of something that is expected and therefore.

Big corporates, especially in South Africa, have this diversity upper hand. So while it's not possible for legacy organisations and their exec teams to mimic or force the energy that comes from start-up culture and the homogenous founder-friends all high-fiving each other for the first few years, it is within the ambit of big corporations to support the thriving of healthy, inspired relationships that have a better chance of surviving the long term. It's just that we cannot expect the HR department to manage this on their own. It must be leader-inspired, -modelled and -led.

Innovation mindsets that can be cultivated and supported in long-term, energetic collectives with good relationships within an organisation, have as much power as any start-up.

4. Growth mindset

The power to see further and do more

The story of how 'growth mindset' made it into our lexicon and understanding goes something like this.

Thirty years ago, psychologist and researcher Carol Dweck became interested in how students reacted to failure and what this said about their mindset. Two significant events happened that helped shape her theory. The first was the startling difference in attitude kids revealed to her when facing a difficult problem she'd presented them with. She recounts the story often in her talks...

"Early in my career I wanted to figure out how kids cope with challenge, so I gave 10 year olds some problems that were a little too difficult for them. Some of them reacted in a shockingly positive way; they said things like 'I love a challenge' or 'I was hoping this would be informative'... but other children, for them it was tragic, catastrophic... their core intelligence had been tested and they were devastated."

The second event played out at a Chicago high school where, Dweck says, she discovered what she calls the "power of yet".

"Students had to pass 84 units to graduate and if they didn't pass they got the grade 'not yet'. I thought, 'Isn't that wonderful?', because if you fail you're nowhere, but if you get the grade 'not yet' you're on a learning curve. 'Not yet' gave them a path into the future."

This was a key moment for Dweck, helping her understand the critical experience she'd had with the kids.

The kids who had responded so well, she says, understood that their abilities could grow through their hard work. In their mindset, it wasn't that they weren't able to do the challenge at all, it's that they weren't able to do it yet. For these kids, intelligence wasn't something they had or didn't have, it was something that they could figure out. Dweck assigned the term 'growth mindset' to this set of perceptions and beliefs.

In contrast, those who'd been gripped by a sense of failure by not getting the challenge at first try were operating from a fixed mindset perspective and were "gripped by the tyranny of now". They didn't innately get that they were able to learn, grow and move beyond their perceived limitations.

The value of the role that mindset plays in our success and growth was surfaced through this work.

To possess a growth mindset means that you don't see failure as the end of all things, but as a springboard to growth and development. It means believing that making mistakes or coming to a dead end doesn't mean there is nothing beyond it.

It means not getting distressed if you don't have the answers, but possessing the curiosity and intrinsic motivation to seek them out. It means that you believe in your ability to become better through hard work and accepting help from others. Of course, this latter skill requires intellectual humility and good relationships to call on. In my experience, this is priceless.

It's not surprising that those kids with a growth mindset behaved in ways that led to greater success.

Dweck is now a leading expert in the field of motivation and is well-known for her work on the mindset as a psychological trait that can be developed. Much like Duckworth and Kiel's beliefs around character, Dweck believes that a growth mindset can be strengthened like a muscle; that simply by believing you can improve your intelligence. Seeing it as a malleable and evolving parameter improves your chances of actually doing so.

"Growth mindset is based on the belief that your basic qualities are things you can cultivate through your efforts", she says. "Although people may differ in every which way in their initial talents and aptitudes, interests, or temperaments, everyone can change and grow through application and experience."

I love how much crossover there is in this field. What I like about the growth mindset character trait is that it encompasses a number of other traits – you have to have the intellectual humility to know that you don't know everything, the other-centredness to look outside yourself for answers. The growth mindset itself takes a kind of grit, the perseverance to see it through, the intrinsic motivation to go beyond an initial hurdle. In fact, it's a big part of Duckworth's unpacking of grit as a trait of the successful.

Over the course of this chapter, I'll be looking at the growth mindset and its importance to you as a leader of an innovation team or process, as well as the role it plays in building that strong ecosystem from the inside out.

The ability to see beyond

If you want a snapshot of why a growth mindset is such a necessary part of being a leader – especially in the field of innovation – just consider this: How many start-ups would've survived their first year if the founders had walked away at the first challenge? Just thought, oh well, it's not within my ambit to deal with this, let me just accept things as they are; let me accept my limitations and the fact that I can't do this now. How many ventures would see the light of day? If I'm honest with you, I've walked away from a fair number within the first year because I've struggled with this particular quality.

Those who want to build something don't just keep going because they're driven by purposeful grit, they persevere because they know they can do better. They can see beyond the now. They can keep learning, keep trying out new projects, keep dealing with failure's lessons, until they find the solution that works for them.

Possessing a growth mindset is fundamental to innovators and those leading the charge in this field because it provides the ability to see beyond failure – to believe there is something to move towards, to be improved on. It's the opposite of expecting perfection and when this doesn't happen, seeing only failure. It's the underlying strength that supports rapid iteration: spinning through the build, measure, learn loop faster than your competitors.

The concept of learning from failure has become common parlance in start-up circles. It really took off in the mainstream in the 2010s and there are countless versions of a sage on a stage recounting their personal experiences of this. It might not be something big corporates are comfortable with in practice (no matter what they say), but anyone in the start-up field with a growth mindset will tell you, failure is an opportunity: an opportunity to learn from mistakes, to grow, to improve and to expand awareness and empathy.

You get the gist of it.

The focus here for me is not so much the reinvention or perception shift on failure, as it is about the ability to trampoline off it. That's the growth mindset. But there is even more value in this trait than this particular face-off against a challenge.

The value of a leadership growth mindset for innovation

As the leader or co-leader of your team of intrapreneurs, or as the lead of your organisation's innovation drive, you absolutely need the capacity to see the big picture. To see beyond the small dips and 'failures' and hold the space for the long-term success. This would seem like the most obvious value of this trait, but cultivating the aspect of growth mindset that 'sees beyond', that sees the 'power of yet', is far-reaching.

1. It helps you kill the zombies

Zombie projects and processes are those living-dead projects that no one seems to be able to just kill off. They go and on, eating everyone's brain energy and annihilating resources. But, due to leadership ego or being enthralled to the sunk cost fallacy (investing in a project because you've invested so much in the project, in other words, throwing good money after bad), no one seems able to just say 'stop'.

In prototyping sessions there is a check-in moment called the 'Pivot, Persist, Kill' session. When you're building trust and validating minimum viable products (or processes for that matter), check-ins help to keep it realistic and validate the resources and funds being allocated to it. These check-ins happen at the end of every stage of the project, and force team members and leaders to ask: Is this working? And if it's not working, what do we do with it? Is our solution almost working but for a small tweak here and there? In which case we pivot. Is our experiment delivering data that affirms our theory? In which case we persist onto the next step. Or is the collected data showing us that our theory, our solution, our MVP, sucks and doesn't work, in which case we kill it off.

Without a growth mindset, without the ability to see beyond, the probability of getting stuck with a zombie project is high. Worse, maybe, would be watching a potential idea die before it's been honed and strengthened and changed into something different, for the better.

2. It helps to motivate your A-Team

It would seem obvious that when you're putting your team together that you'd want to call on the best people in each department within the organisation to join your clever think tank.

But my experience is that the A-Team are not always the right people for this job, because they don't always have a growth mindset. What they're good at doing is figuring out the rules and how to play the game better than anyone else. But the rules are well-established for the status quo game, not innovation of the new. It's one of the reasons that start-ups kick big organisations' ass: people motivated to do only what's been given them to do for their pay-check – or any other expected outcome – aren't likely to rock the boat or be flexible if it means messing with the system.

What interested me about Dweck's research is that kids who are considered talented and intelligent and are praised as such are more likely to be trapped in a fixed mindset and limited by that belief. Research has shown that kids who've been told they're naturally smart limit themselves to challenges that are within their reach. But those 'normal kids' who have to work a little harder? Well, those who've been told about the brain's neuroplasticity and its capacity to learn are more likely to put in the effort when it comes to how they approach tasks and up-skill themselves.

Says Dweck: "Our research shows that when we praise kids for the process they engage in, their hard work, their strategies, their focus, their perseverance, they learn that challenge-thinking, they learn that resilience. Praising talent, praising intelligence, makes them vulnerable."

Those 'naturally smart' people are often unable to reconcile themselves to being beginners. They see the challenge of the new and bail. They're less likely to have the growth mindset and the grit to push through the mental pain barrier of discovering they're not the smartest aleck in the room. People who figure out what the rules are, and then excel at playing them in the game they understand, are not going to be the ones who break any comfort zones. This is at the heart of Duckworth's findings of why people drop out of West Point Military Academy at such an alarming rate: they won't afford themselves the grace to be a beginner during initiation exercises. They've trained their minds and bodies to be top performers for a set task list – not beginners at new challengers that might see them fail.

And that's typically what A-Team players are in organisations... people who excel in the status quo. 'Top performers' are top performers in a game that's well-known to them. Most often, they consider themselves the best and when they're handpicked for any sort of innovation process, they tend to arrive with indifference and arrogance. 'Well of course you've called on me, I'm the best.'

Simply being placed on the team because they're the A-Team can backfire in that it affirms and recognises their position in the status quo. Moreover, they'll be coming into a game they don't know how to play. If they don't have the mindset that can hold this reality, they're not going to be much use to your team.

But that doesn't mean you're going to be on-boarding the problem kids and the shirkers. What you're ultimately looking for are those same people, those 'A-team' employees who excel at being in the status quo, but who have this growth mindset, the ability to unlearn what they're good at, who have the grace to be beginners. The grace to say, "I don't mind being clumsy and bad at something, because I'm intrinsically motivated and I've bought into the think big experience and I'll do whatever it takes".

It's why I always advocate for a recruitment process when putting together innovation or prototyping teams.

Forcing top performers across divisions and positions to apply for a position on the team will reveal those who genuinely want to be part of the process and are intrinsically motivated to get involved in the problem-solving. These are the people who, from a character perspective, are most likely to be willing to act against their own ego needs, learn, listen and be part of the collective.

3.   It helps you see the zero to one

If you're an intrapreneur or a leader managing a team of intrapreneurs, there must be nothing more insufferable to you than the phrase, "But that's the way we've always done it", or "Don't fix what isn't broke".

The title of Thiel's book, *Zero to One*, refers to the ability to create something new – not make incremental changes to existing products, not copy others, but something entirely new to the field.

"Doing what we already know how to do takes the world from one to *n*, adding more of something familiar", Thiel writes. "But every time we create something new, we go from 0 to 1. The act of creation is singular, as is the moment of creation, and the result is something fresh and strange. Unless [business] invests in the difficult task of creating new things, American companies will fail in the future no matter how big their profits remain today."

Sure, it's easy to say that new products and services are so much easier to conjure up if they're the brainchild of one innovative person and brought to life and the market by a small team of entrepreneurs. It's easy to say that legacy corporations aren't capable of harnessing their people's energy the way that start-ups can. But that doesn't mean that legacy organisations have to entrench this as a reality. They simply have to provide the platform and support for their people to get on with it.

Of course, that means changing the organisational culture from a fixed mindset to a growth mindset.

Grendel's mother or the old guard – the leadership and deep systems that ultimately show up as the real innovation hurdle – represent a fixed mindset. This is the mindset that has the system saying, "Oh well, this is the way it's always been done", which has leadership needing to maintain the status quo to maintain their position and discretionary rights.

The more Grendel's Mom – the old guard, the incumbents – seek to keep things as they are, the more they fight against and prevent the growth mindset in themselves and their people, the more the system bogs down, slowing everything needed for innovation.

Rate of learning

In 1828, the chemist, druggist and amateur experimenter John Walker made a mistake. He'd been fiddling about with a combustible paste to be used in percussion caps for the gun trade, when he accidentally scraped the mixing stick against the flagstones of the fireplace. Quite unexpectedly, it "spluttered and caught fire". But instead of putting the flame out and getting back to his original plan, Walker's innovative mind was inspired. He embraced the big idea the accidental scrape had energised, and the friction match was born.

It was a major breakthrough. The ability to control fire with the use of 'friction lights' wherever and whenever needed – without the tiresome process of the tinder box or the danger of chemical matches – changed the face of history.

Fortunately for us but unfortunately for Walker, he was more humanist than entrepreneur. His formula went unpatented as a 'gift to humanity' which meant that although he died penniless, others were able to pick up the idea and improve on it, leaving us with the modern safety match.

Walker displayed something most innovators and inventors are known for: a high rate of learning.

Rate of learning, or ROL, is the speed at which you learn and acquire insights – and how quickly you're able to adapt to the new information and execute based on this.

When Walker made that 'mistake' – scraping an explosive substance against stone – he was able to see the opportunity of the friction itself and adapt to the contextual need. At the time, many aspiring chemists in the new field of science were trying to find a solution to the chemical match, making small tweaks here and there to the composition, but through that happy accident, Walker was able to harness the value of his flash insight and create something entirely new.

His ROL at that moment was high.

When Reis talks about the Long-Term Stock Exchange and the ability to learn and adapt to what matters to your customers and community faster than your competitors can, he's basically talking about ROL. When innovators move through their exploration of customer need and start problem-solving, mocking up MVPs and prototypes, moving through Pivot Persist Kill check points and adapting based on the available data, they're engaging their rate of learning.

There's very little written about this in business literature, but I really like what Kyle Tibbitts has to say about it.

Tibbitts is a start-up jack of all trades, working as a marketing head for Fast, hosting a popular podcast on the topic and supporting fringe Silicon Valley start-ups with advice and angel investing. In 2014, he wrote an article titled, *Rate-of-learning: the most valuable start-up compensation*, which really connected the dots for me. In it he talks about how entrepreneurs need to view ROL as a valuable compensation for the cash they're unlikely to make in their first few years.

"Your rate-of-learning is a better proxy for how successful you will be than your current salary or stock compensation because it's a leading rather than lagging indicator", he writes. "Abandoning the cubicle at your normal job to throw yourself head-first into a start-up is a fiery accelerant for growth, changing your career trajectory by orders of magnitude through a substantially increased rate-of-learning."

As a leader or intrapreneur in a big organisation you might not have the speed or agility to move through processes or make the mistakes that help you learn quickly to really speed up that ROL now, but I believe it's something that needs to be injected into the big corporate culture. And I believe that some corporates really are trying, by putting new systems in place to manage innovation teams or toying with Agile and new ways of working in contained environments that will manage that learning speed and failure/learning rates.

Of course, there's also the individual's capacity for ROL, something that I believe should be exemplified by leaders. There's something to be said for CFOs needing to garner CPD (continuous professional development) points and medical doctors needing to keep their accreditation updated by keeping up to speed with developments in the field. In a way, what this system does is to force or incentivise a growth mindset. It says 'leave your comfortable office and go to this or that industry event or workshop if you wish to stay in your comfortable office'. Why don't we say the same for CEOs or others in the exec team?

The bottom line here for you as a leader is: Are you, in your personal capacity, modelling a growth mindset to your people?

Curiosity and what's next

There's a great opening scene in the animated Dreamworks movie *The Croods*, a story about a Neanderthal family caught between staying as they always have and changing – a crisis point brought to them by a cataclysmic tectonic event and a chance meeting with Guy, an inventive homo sapiens.

In an early scene, one of the main characters, Eep, explains all the ways her father, Grug, has kept them alive with his philosophy 'never not be afraid'. Grug teaches his kids that anything new is bad, curiosity is bad, going out at night is bad... basically anything fun and interesting, unknown and unexplored, is bad and will kill them. And his rules have worked out for them so far. It's kept them alive. But, as Eep says: "That wasn't living, that was just, not dying. There's a difference."

As you can imagine, the arc of the story follows Grug's burgeoning awareness of the world of 'ideas' and gradual acceptance of curiosity and exploration, and how this change in perspective enables him to save his family with the help of intrepid adventurer Guy.

They all live happily ever after.

It's a delightful snapshot of the traditional meeting the new, of how embracing curiosity will drive innovation and discovery. And, honestly, I can read that line by Eep and think of big corporate organisations holding on to traditional ways of working and watching the world change around them until the newbie disruptor comes along and snaps up an opportunity to meet the new world.

Typically, when we thought about the archetypal innovator, curiosity would come up immediately. But time and experience has shown us that great ideas are only worth anything if they're implemented well. As Michael Jordaan says, without this, great ideas are worth nothing. If you've got high curiosity but low grit to bring it to life, you're not going to be a great innovator.

However, like that Marvel Universe I mentioned before, every leadership trait has a role to play in building that innovation ecosystem. They're all linked and you need all the pieces to come together in main or supporting parts for the whole to work optimally. And without curiosity you're not going to be an innovator at all. Without being able to ask the right kinds of questions to conjure up a hundred of those ideas, you're unlikely to land on the one that comes to life. Curiosity is often most alive not in the 'what', but in the 'how the hell are we going to do this?'.

It's curiosity that motivates innovators to ask the questions that pave the way to answers. If chemist and amateur innovator John Walker hadn't asked himself *how* he might harness the power of the friction he'd seen at work with the mixing stick, who knows how much longer it would've taken to perfect the freedom of easy, convenient moveable 'fire starters'.

It's curiosity that drives leaders to continually seek out the new ideas, people, services and processes that will keep their organisations tracking change, attracting customers and staying ahead of competitors. It's curiosity that drives them to bring ideas to life. This innovation effort often dwarfs the innovation prowess of the original idea, which almost always turns out to have been a terrible one.

I've placed curiosity within the growth mindset bucket because it's the trait that enables us to keep expanding ourselves, to further our line of sight after we've seen beyond the challenge. It's curiosity that allows us to keep going with the questions, "What if we tried something new?", "Where can I improve on this outcome?" and "How might we serve our customers better?".

It's curiosity that allows the exploration of possibility.

How to be curious

Curiosity is still something of an enigma to researchers. Bundled under the catch-all phrase 'information finding', which serves our evolution, it can also be a seemingly pointless pursuit of idle wondering that comes with high risk for long-term learning. For example, someone in our history must've wondered if they could eat a red-cap mushroom and then popped it into their mouth for a little taste.

Then there's the matter of how curiosity exists physically in humans. There are theories that centre genetics, explaining why some people have a greater talent for it than others, like having a musical skill or flair for numbers. One explanation attributes it to neoteny – the evolutionary theory that means the "retention of juvenile characteristics".

Tom Stafford is a cognitive scientist at the University of Sheffield. In a piece for the BBC, he writes: "Evolution, by making us a more juvenile species, has made us weaker than our primate cousins, but it has also given us our child's curiosity, our capacity to learn and our deep sense of attachment to each other."

The young child's questioning of 'why, why, why' is the insatiable seeking out of information, the passionate dedication to knowing more for knowing's sake, to establish a kind of social proprioception and place oneself in a system alongside others. To access this as an adult means to be able to access that inner child; to inspire that childlike quality in oneself. The part of you that understands there is more to know in the world, to learn and explore, that understands there are others who have knowledge you don't, that gifts you the capacity to acknowledge that there is a world of people, insights and experiences that you are a stranger to and that hold value.

Yet again, it's hardly the stuff business school is made of. And yet again, it really should be.

Francesca Gino is a professor at Harvard Business School. She's the author of *Rebel Talent: Why it Pays to Break the Rules in Work and Life* and is a behavioural scientist in the psychology of organisations, focusing specifically on how people can lead more productive, creative and fulfilling lives. In a paper for Harvard Business School, *The Business Case for Curiosity*, she notes research that shows curiosity leads to "higher-performing, more-adaptable firms".

"Curiosity is much more important to an enterprise's performance than was previously thought", she says. "That's because cultivating it at all levels helps leaders and their employees adapt to uncertain market conditions and external pressures: When our curiosity is triggered, we think more deeply and rationally about decisions and come up with more-creative solutions."

Gino believes that curiosity also allows leaders to "gain more respect from their followers" and "inspires employees to develop more trusting and more collaborative relationships with colleagues".

So why isn't leadership curiosity more of conversation starter?

For leaders, especially those in hostile corporate environments, it can be hard to be vulnerable enough to say, "I don't know". And asking peers and employees, "What do you think?" might feel like an admonition of a character flaw or skills failing. It's one of the trappings of that highest paid position to believe you're supposed to know everything.

This trapping of leadership limitation ends up filtering through the organisational culture. Of the 3,000 Gino surveyed, "only about 24% reported feeling curious in their jobs on a regular basis, and about 70% said they face barriers to asking more questions at work". The reasons for this are complex, she says. Leaders feel exploration will be costly and upset the status quo; that it isn't efficient enough.

Interestingly, Enron's catch phrase was 'Ask why', yet when someone started asking 'why', their house of cards collapsed.

As a leader, it's your job to model curiosity in the workplace, but you can't hold the power of the childlike 'why' and intellectual superiority at the same time. They're mutually exclusive concepts. To embrace the curious mindset, you first need to embrace intellectual humility, collaboration, and respect for and trust in your peers and employees. You don't need to know everything. You can ask. You can engage. You can ask intelligent questions. Gino cites Greg Dyke, director general of the BBC, asking staff, "What is the one thing I should do to make things better for you?" when he joined in 2000.

This might run counter to the human-centred design logic that you should never ask the customer what they want, but rather develop empathy for their pains and experiment with solutions to address the most pressing of these. But empathy sessions are in themselves always questioning and empathy interviews deliver all the insight needed to fully understand the problem space.

When it comes to fostering and embedding a culture of curiosity with your people, she suggests hiring for curiosity (in particular the 'T-shaped employee'), modelling inquisitiveness by asking curious questions, emphasising and encouraging learning and broadening your employees' minds, and finally setting up 'Why' and 'How Might We' days.

How might we...

"To encourage curiosity, leaders should also teach employees how to ask good questions", says Gino. "Organising 'Why?' days, when employees are encouraged to ask that question if facing a challenge, can go a long way toward fostering curiosity."

It's similar to what the innovation sphere will know as hackathon days or blitzes or workshops – time-boxed spaces for problem solvers to really ask the big questions.

As is good practice, I regularly kick off my work with clients using How Might We challenge-framing blitzes. 'How Might We' is a classic Design Thinking activity to reframe the problem at hand and start mining that collective wisdom for solutions. The process gets everyone aligned around what challenge really is and provides boundaries for teams to innovate within. But it also opens up the floor for these curious possibilities and avenues – all of which are unearthed by the question 'How might we?' How might we better serve our clients? How might we become the market-leading retailer? How might we encourage learning among our employees?

In whichever format I work with clients, it's always going to be about the questions. I'm much more interested in good questions than having good answers. I don't want to have the best answers in the room – I want the best questions in the room. The moment you say you know 100%, is the moment you stop learning.

Curiosity for the people

One the other reasons I really enjoyed Gino's paper was that it looked at how the entire employee base of an organisation could be inspired. Gino outlines the many ways that businesses tap into their employees' curiosity with genuinely innovative results. In fact, a 2018 *Innovation-By-All Report* by Great Place to Work demonstrates that organisations that invite all employees into the innovation process achieve "5.5 times the revenue growth of peers with a less inclusive approach to innovation".

It's been validating to get confirmation that 'innovation specialists' don't have the monopoly on the right answer, that tapping into the collective of the existing workforce is enough, because I see it in my practice all the time. I've learned that the real heroes of innovation are in the back office, especially when it comes to services and new ways of working. The people who really manage to get innovations to stand up and scale are all the ops people – they're the unsexy opposite of the razzle-dazzle polo neck visionaries. They're really where the magic of implementation happens and they don't get enough credit. If you're smart enough to include them in ideation workshops, they're usually the people asking the pain-in-the-arse questions and highlighting the potholes in flight of fancy imaginings. This might feel frustrating to those unfamiliar with the messy work of innovation and implementation, but if teams are coached well in the language of plussing and curious questions, they can be some of your most valuable assets.

Each and every time it reminds me that the superstars of innovation, those polo neck-wearing cowboys and 'visionaries' –are not the only people to look to when creating a solid innovation ecosystem juiced with curiosity and creativity. Real systems changes and innovations can result from tapping into your existing employee base's curiosity. You don't need to create an 'innovation office' staffed by specialist 'innovators'.

Creativity

In 1965, a nine-year-old boy read Arthur C. Clarke's *Dial F for Frankenstein* in the January issue of *Playboy* magazine. Clarke's story imagines a world where telephones form a vast, complex, interconnected network, becoming a giant consciousness that first creates chaos with local moms and then turns on the world and destroys everything we know and love. In 1989, that little boy, now 25 years old, became the father of the World Wide Web. The vast, complex, interconnected information system that provides the binary highway for the internet.

Tim Berners-Lee has since been knighted, called the modern-day Gutenberg and sits on every board that controls the Web and its continuous development. In a 2001 *Time* article about his life's work, he recalls Clarke's *Dial F for Frankenstein:* "It's... about 'crossing the critical threshold of number of neurons', about 'the point where enough computers get connected together' that the whole system 'started to breathe, think, react autonomously'."

Clarke is not the only author to have been credited for their works of science fiction inspiring real-world inventors and their inventions.

Jules Verne's 1870 *Twenty Thousand Leagues Under the Sea* captivated the inventor of the modern submarine, Simon Lake. Martin 'Marty'

Cooper of Motorola, world-recognised inventor of the portable cell phone, considered Dick Tracy's 1946 two-way wrist radio one of the seminal triggers for his inspiration. And the inventor of the taser, NASA physicist Jack Cover, was a fan of the fictional character Tom Swift. 'Taser' is an acronym for one the inventions found in the book *Thomas A. Swift's Electric Rifle*.

The list goes on...

QuickTime was the brainchild of Steve Perlman, the Apple scientist who got the idea while watching an episode of *Star Trek: The Next Generation*, where one of the characters listens to multiple music tracks on his computer. And the online community Second Life? Its inventor Philip Rosedale says he was inspired by Neal Stephenson's 1992 novel *Snow Crash*, which presents an immersive 'metaverse' where people interact with one another through 'avatars'. And on and on... Star Trek's Universal Translators and then Google Translate; replicators and then 3D printing...

Creativity is not the skill to paint nicely or string a few sentences together. It's the ability to generate or recognise ideas, possibilities and alternatives; the ultimate capacity to suspend belief in what is to imagine what could be – without judgement or limitations. Looking at just the few examples above, the relationship between creativity (idea generation) and innovation (idea implementation) is clear. (One could say the next step in this process is entrepreneurship: taking it to market and capitalising on the opportunities).

Ultimately, what you're looking to do is to inspire this kind of innate curiosity and creativity in your people. In 2016, the WEF predicted that creativity would be one of the top three quintessential skills needed in 2020, along with complex problem-solving and critical thinking. As we make our way through the start of the 4th Industrial Revolution, human creativity will be where we are most likely to excel and one the areas it's worth fostering in your workforce.

This isn't to say that every single person is going to have the same capacity to visualise and imagine, but what you're looking to do is to support the creative process, which will in turn build collaboration, foster trust and inspire engagement – all those juicy elements needed to attract and retain your talent and keep productivity high.

Yes and...

In Design Thinking workshops, getting the best from the collective means inspiring the collective growth mindset and its related qualities of creativity and curiosity. Not every individual will be willing or initially available to the idea; not everyone will be skilled in the process. But, trust me, the collective will eventually bring them along and the collaborative process will work its magic. It never fails.

One of the ways I coach for and get some alignment in the creative space is through plussing.

'Plussing' was reportedly invented by Walt Disney, who used the technique to make an idea even better. Whenever his animators thought they'd nailed a scene, Disney would ask them to find a way to make it even better. Later, the studio would expand this to their theme parks: what more could they do for the customer, what expectations could they excel... In Pixar's heyday, head honcho Randy Nelson talked about using improv techniques and plussing to work collaboratively and get the best ideas from his team. It allowed his creatives to listen actively, demonstrate respect for each other and the ideas on offer, remain curious and get involved.

I use plussing a lot in my workshops to get the collective on board with the creative process. In particular, I use the improv technique 'Yes, and'. The concept is simply to 'plus' any idea that is presented by accepting it without judgement, adding to it and making your thinking partners feel good.

 So, for example, Person A starts off with a basic statement and everyone in the group expands this with a 'yes and' statement. It can work just as easily with two people.

Person A: Let's go to the beach...
Person B: ...yes and let's take the beach bats...
Person C: ...yes and let's invite Jean and Bob...
Person D: ...yes and let's have a braai afterwards...

And so on and so on. Now you have a whole day of adventures opening to you. Far better than:

Person A: Let's go to the beach...
Person B: Nah, it'll be too much hassle.

Now replace the beach with product or service ideas and suddenly the possibilities open wide up:

Person A: Let's provide a coffee station in our retail store....
Person B: ...Yes and let's put in some benches for our customers to relax...
Person C: ...Yes and let's provide some light snacks...
Person D: ...Yes and let's...

Suddenly you have the possibility of an entirely new revenue stream.

It's a very basic exercise with a very big pay-off, especially within groups of people who may not be used to getting the platform to tap into their creativity. Similarly, during feedback and iterating sessions, I use a technique called 'I like, I wish, I wonder'. It's a plussing phrase that helps to structure feedback positively and help each team member contribute meaningfully and build on what has been presented.

Creativity responds to context

Here's the thing about creativity though: it can't flourish in fear. Unfortunately, this is the atmosphere in which most people at big corporates operate. More unfortunate is the fact that a lot of drive for 'innovation' in these spaces – anything like looks and smells like innovation, no matter how much theatre it is – is motivated by fear.

When I was brought in as an innovation lead at one of the major banking houses in South Africa, one of the mistakes I made was to jump into the rhetoric that we're going to get taken out by fintechs. We were going to be the buffalo that dies from a million mosquito bites. It's in the same WhatsApp group as 'incumbents getting taken out by the disruptors'; that big business better watch its step because the little guys were going to be snapping at that Achilles heel and taking over their business.

Now we know that if the big guys are smart enough, they know when to bring those disruptors into their fold. We also know that if the big guys are smart enough, they'll know it's time to change their ecosystems. But even this more often than not inspires fear, not excitement.

I'd talk to line managers about new ways of working, saying that you're going to have to reinvent who you are and the role that you play and you have to be much more egalitarian and be prepared to sit at the table with graduates and work as equals and all that stuff – that doesn't inspire them. It shuts their brains down to the possibilities because they get pissed off or scared about what that means for them.

You can't scare or anger people into being inspired to solve problems, yet we've been primed to fear from the first entrance into the education system.

In Ken Robinson's TED Talk about kids and creativity, 'Do schools kill creativity?', he talks about how, from the moment we step into a school, we're taught that being creative is valued below being wired for maths or languages, and to fear mistakes and being wrong.

"[But] what we do know is, if you're not prepared to be wrong, you'll never come up with anything original... And by the time they get to be adults, most kids have lost that capacity. They have become frightened of being wrong. And we run our companies like this. We stigmatize mistakes. And we're now running national education systems where mistakes are the worst thing you can make. And the result is that we are educating people out of their creative capacities."

Listening to this talk again, I was reminded of a piece of behind-the-scenes footage in Peter Jackson's new docu-series *The Beatles: Get Back*. In the clip, we see Paul McCartney in studio on his guitar riffing by himself as he tries to come up with a song for the album they're putting together. As he works his way through and around chords and half-melodies, there are off-notes and dead-ends, weird progressions and nonsense warbles. Of course, none of this stops him continuing. None of the rubbishy sounds give him pause or make anyone in the studio around him raise an eyebrow. And then slowly, slowly you hear it emerge: the tune to *Get Back*. What you see created 'in real time' is one of their later big hits –

and you hear the messiness that it was born from. If McCartney had been stopped by shame or embarrassment at the first bum note he made on the way, *Get Back* would never have been created.

Is it possible in your organisation?

We know that if you work on your creativity you build empathy, and if you build empathy you can deepen your purpose. If you can deepen your purpose, you can access grit. If you can access a long-term view, you can work on your growth mindset, which gets you curious about adapting, and so on and so on. This stuff is all connected.

The process of fostering creativity is the same process as fostering trust, and a sense of psychological safety in the workspace is the same process as building good relationships. As a leader in the organisation, is it possible for you to work more creatively and to foster that creativity in your workforce? Why not? Dweck's belief that a growth mindset could be fostered is based on brain plasticity or 'neuroplasticity' – the 'ability of neural networks in the brain to change through growth and reorganisation'. In other words, the capacity for your very synapses to change through learning and function. Much like grit, your growth mindset and creativity can literally be cultivated, practiced and strengthened, but for it to flourish, it needs a space free from fear of failure or making mistakes.

5. Empathy

Going where few business leaders dare to tread

In *Voyager,* the fifth series of the Star Trek franchise, Robert Picardo plays The Doctor, an Emergency Medical Holographic programme that must step in when the crew's human doctor is killed by a powerful energy wave (you know, as is so often the case in space). Much like the AI character Data in *The Next Generation,* The Doctor becomes the show's enquiry into what it means to be human. One of his first moments of awakening happens early in the second season with an experience that introduces him to one of the traits that define our humanity: empathy.

In the B-plot of the episode *Tattoo*, The Doctor goes about his business as usual, dismissing his patients' aches and pains as "whiny, cranky attitudes". Dismayed by his lack of compassion, his assistant Kes accuses him of being unsympathetic.

"I wish once in your life you could know how it makes you feel vulnerable", Kes exclaims, "then you'd understand".

But The Doctor is unmoved. He can't understand the human experience because he hasn't been programmed to feel pain or discomfort and cannot suffer the way humanoids do. Nevertheless, always up for a challenge and determined to set an example of grittiness, The Doctor programmes himself with a case of 'Levodian flu' and all its attendant symptoms: fever, fatigue, sneezing, coughing, aches and pains. Of course, 30 hours later he's reduced to a vulnerable, piteous, snivelling mess and becomes a terrible patient, whining for attention, begging for Kes not to leave him alone, fearful of dying...

The result of the experiment? Instant empathy, compassion and flexibility for the lived experience of his patients. In the long run, it made him an even better doctor than the simple diagnostician he'd been programmed to be.

The Doctor reminds me of Kiehl's psycho CEOs and their lack of capacity to connect with the people around them. This is hardly an anomaly across the corporate culture spectrum. The topic of empathy is basically the outer limits of known space in traditional business; a dreaded blackhole zone of the 'touchy-feely' stuff that's best left to HR or, frankly, each employee's personal development with their own therapist. I think it's fair to generalise that for most industry leaders, whether they're empathetic or not isn't really a concern for them. At best, it might be a momentary thought-provoking read from Brené Brown or Adam Grant on a LinkedIn post. After all, it's not as necessary a skillset as, say, an MBA FCCA CFA when it comes to the really serious business of putting numbers on the page and ensuring good shareholder payouts, or getting bums on seats and feet through the door.

Except that it is.

Over the course of this short chapter, I'll be looking at how empathy is often a key ingredient in effective innovation – not only to better understand your client base and how you might be better able to solve their most pressing their needs in the future, but how it benefits your team cohesion and morale.

However, before we get to more of that...

What is empathy exactly?

Philosophers and psychologists have been trying to unpack the exact nature of empathy for centuries. For early English philosophers and students of the human condition, the concept of 'empathy' was wrapped up in that of 'sympathy'. In fact, it was only in 1908 that the German psychological term *Einfühlung*, 'feeling in', found its way into the English lexicon as 'empathy'; the ability to not only understand another's situation, like one might with sympathy, but to share and feel their experience. It's how you might 'walk a mile in their shoes' without leaving your armchair, why you might cry if you see your daughter sad, why you might feel overwhelmed with delight at seeing someone you love genuinely happy.

How this emotional or physiological state-matching (seeing your sadness makes me feel sad for your sadness, your laughing with delight makes me laugh with delight) finds a place in our evolution is a complex scientific discussion best suited to those researchers who know what they're talking about. However, extremely simply put for our purposes, it's theorised that empathy finds its roots in much the same place our other quality traits do: creating and maintaining relationships, safety and societal equilibrium. It's a long-evolved trait that requires some serious higher-level brain functioning.

Razia Sahi, a psychology researcher focusing on the connection between the social world and emotion regulation, sums it up best for me in her piece for *Psychology in Action* (my italics): "When we empathise with someone, we use cognitive processes to try to *understand* their emotional state and *imagine* ourselves in that state by drawing on our own emotional memories, ultimately *embodying* the emotions that we are imagining."

And there are nuances to empathy.

The clever people who study these sorts of things have divided the trait into two forms, essentially: cognitive empathy and emotional or affective empathy. Cognitive empathy is the ability to see from another's perspective and recognise their thoughts and feelings – to be able imagine yourself into their experience. Emotional or affective empathy is the ability to respond to that with the appropriate emotion and even action. This latter form of empathy is quite a lot easier to slip into when you're dealing with people you already care for. For example, your partner suffers a terrible grief or pain, and you find yourself crying or trying to make their life easier. However, when it comes to people outside of your intimate circles, such as your peers, customers or employees, cognitive empathy becomes the muscle you strengthen to better relate to them and, in the context of our work here, to strengthen your business.

Empathy, people and innovation

If you've touched on human-centred design in the problem-solving or innovation space, you'll have come across 'empathy' quite often. It's used as a design principle that participants engage with through a well-facilitated process to understand the problem space better. Over the course of a workshop or sprint, for example, you'll be familiarised with a framework that will teach you how to exercise your cognitive empathy muscles by putting yourself in the shoes of the people who matter most to your success, whether they are stakeholders or customers.

Consultants and agencies will personalise this framework and give it all sorts of names, but the basis of the empathy process remains the same: to truly understand who your customer is, how they experience their context, and what their pains and needs are. The idea, ultimately, is to ensure that your team is solving the right problem – the most pressing one from the perspective of your customer. You'll do this so that you might find ways of solving for their real pains and needs, thereby serving them better, and, in so doing, remaining relevant to your market base which will, ultimately, make you a buck or two. That's the quick version about why empathy for your external customers' pains might matter to your business.

But the truth is, as always, more meaningful and pervasive than that. Empathy matters beyond 'just' providing the right product or service or solution to your client base. It also matters how you perceive your business and how you lead your people and teams. And because of that, it matters to the long-term success of your venture, far beyond just making it through another financial year.

Empathy and your 'internal customer'

Empathy for your external customers is technically easy: explore the problem space with empathy to understand your customer's needs so that you can supply a better product or a service. The benefits of using this framework are so obvious it's crazy that more companies aren't doing it as a matter of course. And yet, this shouldn't be surprising to me. Because although it's technically an 'easy' process, what it reveals is sometimes far more complex for the organisation to digest.

In all the empathy sessions I've facilitated, it's remarkable how the external customer's happiness and user experience almost aways comes down to the internal customer's happiness and user experience of the business itself.

As legacy organisations start the gargantuan task of shifting and innovating systems to more modern ways of working, they're coming face to face with a reality traditional leaders and organisational systems have tried to ignore: people matters *in* the business matter *to* the business. And this stretches far beyond how many days of leave employees get or how much of a cash bonus they can expect for the extra work they put in to improve the company's bottom line.

The value of empathy in the ecosystem

Empathy is a regular bullet point in conversations around transformational or servant leadership. In these circles, there's a lot about 'leading from within' in ways that affect real organisational change and so on, but the basics are essentially this: empathy is your ability to be human to other humans – regardless of where you see yourself on the ladder of power.

In the 'leadership character as culture' equation, empathy is about finding your humanity in what has been, up until now, a largely inhumane system. Today, human beings in an organisation are often still referred to as 'resources' and 'capital'; objects simply to be moved and removed as the capitalist system sees fit. Of course business and marketplace necessities require all sorts of shifts that often affect employees at the coal face the hardest, but *how* your organisation shifts and *how* you communicate those shifts is where empathy becomes the differentiating factor between traditional and modern leadership.

There's a validation of someone's humanity – and yours – when you approach your people and their context with empathy. And it works. Studies are confirming the positive effect that leadership empathy has on the individuals and teams that work within this culture. What I cover below is hardly the full extent of these, but the following points are where I've seen empathy benefit and build a culture of continuous innovation.

Empathy supports progress over perfection

Embracing the human journey means to embrace failure as learning – an integral part of the process of becoming a better entity. In innovation we think of this as iterating – refining ideas and prototypes in small steps, picking up weaknesses, improving strengths and so on until we get a final product that answers the problem we have in the best way possible.

One of the greatest examples of this at work in an ecosystem is *kaizen*, a Japanese business philosophy meaning 'change for the better' or 'continuous improvement'. It embraces continuously improving operations and, importantly, involving all employees in the process. It's the ultimate antidote to 'it's the way we've always done it'. Toyota famously adopted the philosophy in their business, encouraging and empowering its employees to identify problem areas and possible solutions.

Kaizen and iterating is about efficiency and effectiveness, but importantly it's about taking everyone who opts in and their inputs and ideas into account, thereby building engagement and a team atmosphere, making people feel heard and part of the system. Everyone at every level is considered. Every 'failure' is a learning.

What I like about the concept of *kaizen* in particular, is that it bakes the concept of iteration into the whole business, understanding that there is never one totally perfect expression of the organisation, but a continually growing, less mechanistic, more organic and ultimately more agile and flexible system. One that recognises the humans at the heart of a business.

Getting the best out of your people

We now know that a lack of ability, resources and motivation are a few of the top contributors to poor performance. Traditionally, we've thought of these along linear lines only within the confines of the physical company – not having the resources, the funds, the tech, the team, the time etc. to complete a task or suitable motivation such as bonuses to excel. But what do ability, resources and motivation mean in a country like South Africa, where education standards are dwindling and people's personal, daily struggles are so intimately connected to the national.

As I write this, the pandemic is going endemic in the midst of our country's devastating economic situation: we're in the middle of rolling electricity and water blackouts, public transport has been eroded, the petrol price is at an all-time high, blatantly corrupt politicians continue to avoid criminal prosecution, and official crime statistics show that the number of rapes, domestic violence and child murders has risen yet again. It's dire.

For the bulk of our employees, simply getting to work is a struggle. Staying motivated to innovate at work when it feels like so much is breaking while you're constantly broke, hungry and afraid for the safety of your children is impossible – but millions of South African frontline workers do it anyway.

The challenges we face in this country have deep historical roots. Colonial and apartheid laws excluded black people, women, people living with disabilities, and other marginalised groups from fully participating in the South African education system and labour market. Apartheid socially engineered black poverty so successfully that the rates of systemic economic inequality reflected along racial lines continue to grow decades after its collapse. Internet access also reflects racial and economic inequality, and having an aspirational device at home in an impoverished township can put your family at risk for crime, while the luxury of a room with a door that closes during remote video calls is also not a possibility for most South African employees.

If this is the situation on any normal business-as-usual kind of day, what might this mean for cultivating an innovation mindset within your people to build an agile and responsive ecosystem for your business? The ability to speak up, ideate and experiment requires enormous courage within a volatile macro context. As a leader trying to build that innovation mindset in your people, empathy and understanding for the very real stressors they face every day is the only way you will be able to get the best out of them.

It collapses the gap

Diversity has been more than a buzzword in corporate South Africa for decades now; it's been a legislative imperative and a competitive advantage to understanding our country's wildly varied marketplace.

As remote working becomes ubiquitous and digital workplaces cross borders and continents, the need to find common ground becomes critical. Beyond embracing diversity as a constitutional imperative, it becomes a business, socio-economic and moral imperative. But while diversity comes with its advantages, it also comes with a learning curve for the individuals in the team interacting with each other and for the leader of the team managing this diversity.

As the one setting that culture, it's incumbent on the leader and leadership teams to set the tone for engagement and interaction when the inevitable conflicts or misunderstandings arise. One way to manage any dissonance that might come up for you is a strong empathy trait.

"Empathy allows us to bridge the gap between how we see things and how others experience them", writes leadership expert Tanveer Naseer. "Through our empathy, we're able to move beyond the binary attitude of ' I'm right/you're wrong' which can impede any initiative from moving forward, to one that's driven by the desire to discover that common ground we share with one another so that we can promote collaboration and foster sustainable growth."

What I like so specifically about this bridging the binary 'I'm right/you're wrong' gap is how well it applies to collapsing the hierarchy – the HIPPO versus the little guy – during an innovation process or in building that ecosystem. Even in something as basic as an ideation session, its ability to level the playing field is invaluable – in this space everyone's input is valid and valuable, everyone has a contribution to make.

Naseer rightly points out that the key to an organisation's success is no longer based solely on the processes and technologies found within your company's walls, "but within the talents, insights, and experiences of those you lead", which he says is something you can only tap into "if we create conditions where people feel connected to what they do and to those around them, as well as being a part of the shared purpose that defines your collective efforts".

Empathy and your leadership capacity

Over the course of his study into character and leadership, Kiel came to outline the three habits that the virtuoso CEOs displayed. The first is what he calls the empathy habit – the ability to be able to sense what other people are feeling. For virtuoso CEOs, he says, this is a core competency. "You were born with a perfect skill in doing this, but growing up in our culture it's probably often been trained out of you. You've probably also been told that in our culture business is business and don't get personally involved in business decisions, right? Well, wrong if you're a virtuoso CEO. They get involved in personal relationships..."

Before I move on to the second and third habits, I'd like to pause a moment here to touch on what Kiel's saying about this cultural unlearning of empathy. In 2004, Simon Baron-Cohen and Sally Wheelwright, researchers at the Autism Research Centre at the University of Cambridge, developed the Empathy Quotient, a self-reporting instrument they had created to measure empathy in individuals. Fast-forward to 2018 and the largest genetic study of empathy ever undertaken. A multi-disciplinary collaboration comprising Baron-Cohen and the Cambridge team, genetics company 23andMe and a team of international scientists, employed more than 46,000 23andMe customers to complete the 80-point Empathy Quotient questionnaire online (it's easily available, in case you're interested) and then send in a saliva sample for analyses.

For our purposes, an interesting thing emerged from the study. Although there was some indication of genetic predisposition for empathy, mostly in that the genetic variants associated with lower empathy were also associated with higher risk for autism, it was clear that this genetic variant doesn't extend to the sex of the individual. Although the study confirmed that women are, on average, more empathetic than men, this wasn't due to genes but rather, among other things, non-biological factors such as socialisation.

In other words, your upbringing, experience and the mores of the day that dictate gender roles and influence how you're expected to behave as a woman or a man – 'girls like pink and are more caring', 'boys like blue and don't have feelings', that sort of thing – is more likely to affect your capacity for empathy than your genes might.

Taking that back to Kiel's observations, it makes me reflect on how we might've been trained for business or even leadership. Research has shown us that people in the medical profession exhibit decreasing levels of empathy the more experienced they become, so why would people leading the historically dehumanising capitalist system be any different? And is there a way to unlearn what we've been taught about the cold and dehumanising requirement of business leaders and learn how to build that empathy muscle to maximise the benefits not only for yourself, your team and business, but for the wider community?

As for Kiel's second and third habits of virtuoso CEOs, they really follow in the wake of the first and speak to other traits already covered.

His second is the 'Others First' habit, which in my mind falls within the other-centredness trait. "When virtuoso CEOs make a significant business decision the first thing they think about is how is this going to impact other people and what's best for other people what's best for the business... it's never about me and my salary or my status."

His third habit is what he calls the 'I screwed up' habit, when leaders admit to their mistakes. When they do so, he says, it frees their people up to explore. "When a leader admits to making a mistake it communicates trust and respect for people in the room that you're talking to. It's an equaliser." There's that intellectual humility, that trust, that relationship building. It's all connected.

We know that character traits can be built on and strengthened. We know how valuable it is for better business and innovation. But we also know that empathy is one of the traits being weakened in the current social set-up.

A well-known University of Michigan study analysed data gathered from almost 14,000 students between 1979 and 2009, and found there was a more than 48% drop in empathy compared to 30 years ago, with the bulk of the decline happening from 2000 – at about the same time the internet and social media really started off. You could argue that this is one university in one state in one country, but the WEF's 2019 *Global Risk Report* cited this Michigan study under a new report section called 'Heads and Hearts: The Human Side of Global Risk'.

Declining psychological and emotional well-being is a risk in itself, says the report, affecting the wider global risks landscape. "Anger is increasing and empathy appears to be in decline", is the gist of it, with the internet, tech, automation, monitoring and a loss of personal control by the individual being some of the greatest drivers. Should this matter to you as business leader? Should empathy? You bet. "The global economic impact of mental disorders in 2010 was US$2.5 trillion with indirect costs (lost productivity, early retirement and so on) outstripping direct costs (diagnosis and treatment) by a ratio of about 2:1", says the report. "If empathy were to continue to decline the risks might be even starker."

Practicing empathy

If empathy has been flagged as a point of growth for you, don't feel alone. As we've seen, inherent affective empathy is often socialised out of men and beaten out of some professions, and cognitive empathy is hard work, especially if you haven't necessarily worked that muscle enough or at all. It's not exactly the trait supported by tech and social media, and for modern leaders working in a traditional system it's certainly not a trait that's been encouraged. Frankly, given the trying circumstances modern business finds itself in, the pressure to detach can be overwhelming. As a leader in any size business or division, you're the one carrying the emotional weight of the people in your team. It's an additional stress that you may or may not acknowledge.

But there is a long-term view to consider here. If you want to create a legacy or build the business you're in by supporting new ways of working and inspiring your people to get collaborative and creative, to trust you enough to bring their best selves to work and to buy into your organisation's purpose, you're going to have to pull finger on tapping into the touchy feelies.

Unfortunately, becoming more empathetic isn't as easy as simply loading 'Levodian Flu' as a subroutine to your matrix and suddenly catching feelings for your fellow humans. Your own personal research into how you can build this muscle will lead you down all sorts of avenues, and there is a vast field of work to tap into to learn. But I've found these next few points to be the most relevant to the innovation space.

Get a mentor

There's not a strong culture of mentorship around different aspects and dimensions of innovation, and learning empathy should be no different. I like what Russell Brand once had to say about mentors: Find mentors not because they live a perfect life, but because there's an aspect or dimension of their life that you want to work on that they were good at. Find a couch or mentor who is comfortable with feelings and talking honestly about them; someone who you can touch base with about what empathy in the workplace might look like and feel like.

Learn how to listen

This really comes back to the 'great relationships' piece. As a facilitator, I've had to learn how to do this myself and it's a really big part of creating a safe space people can trust. This speaks somewhat to the earlier mention of how exposing this kind of radical problem-solving work can feel. If you're always asserting your opinion, disregarding inputs, speaking over people or misinterpreting the information they're providing, you're going to struggle to get your team to open up and produce their best work. Asking simple questions such as 'What do you think?' or 'How do you feel about XYZ?', and accepting the feedback or insights without judgement, is a valuable start to practicing empathy with the humans in your team.

Show appreciation

For a long time, extrinsic motivators such as corporate innovation awards were considered super important to driving innovation in an organisation. The idea was a simple social feedback loop: those who achieve some form of excellence in their field are acknowledged with an award, thereby encouraging further innovation and inspiring the creative spirit in would-be innovators and so on. An added bonus was that these awards made the organisation itself appear innovative by association.

Unfortunately, it seems none of these glitzy awards do very much but provide cashflow for the hospitality industry.

In a 2017 paper for the *International Journal of Innovation Management*, *Innovation awards: Reward, Recognition, and Ritual*, authors Lisa Callagher and Peter Smith write: "Awards may even reduce intrinsic motivation by shifting the focus from the work to the award. Other negative consequences include frustration and demotivation if the awards are poorly administered, a focus of obtaining the award with the least possible effort, or even detracting from the quality of the work by focusing on the award instead."

Even monetary compensation might have unintended consequences. Researchers from the London School of Economics conducted an analysis of 51 experiments into performance-related incentives and found that these could actually backfire. Says Dr Bernd Irlenbusch of the LSE's Department of Management: "We find that financial incentives may indeed reduce intrinsic motivation and diminish ethical or other reasons for complying with workplace social norms such as fairness."

Daniel H. Pink wrote about this in his 2011 book, *Drive: The Surprising Truth About What Motivates Us*, arguing that these extrinsic motivators – the carrot, the target bonus, the award – used to work for repetitive and rule-specific jobs in the 20th century (e.g. complete this many products on a manufacturing line and get this much bonus), but this isn't what works today where tasks require creativity and problem solving. Pink's solution is a three-pillar system that encourages intrinsic motivation, namely autonomy (the urge to direct our own lives), mastery (the desire to get better at something that matters) and purpose (the yearning to do what we do in the service of something larger than ourselves). Pink talks about enabling and supporting employees to attain these three pillars: the flexibility and trust, building relationships (this should all start looking very familiar at this point), affording time, empowerment, upskilling, servant leadership, purpose... everything that feeds in to support the intrinsic motivation that drives creativity and innovation. Of course, this isn't to say that money doesn't matter. Pink points to 'baseline rewards' such as contracts, salary, benefits and perks, and assumes that people are paid fairly and adequately. It's just that these simply don't inspire loyalty, trust or intrinsic motivation. But there's another facet that I've found best exemplified by Mike Robbins.

Robbins is the author of *Bring Your Whole Self to Work*, in which he focuses his attention on the value of bringing humanity to leadership roles. What I enjoyed about his take on reward is his take on appreciation. Robbins draws a distinction between recognition and appreciation. The former, he says, is performance-based and conditional, limited, top-down and retrospective, while appreciation "is about acknowledging a person's inherent value... The point isn't their accomplishments. It's their worth as a colleague and a human being". In short, he says, recognition is about what people do; appreciation is about who they are.

This is particularly interesting in terms of big change and innovation processes. If you're only recognising the positives, it's going to be rough riding when the failures, dips and messy moments inevitably happen. "If you focus solely on praising positive outcomes, on recognition", says Robbins, "you miss out on lots of opportunities to connect with and support your team members – to appreciate them".

Robbins goes some way in unpacking how to appreciate your people and it's a valuable avenue of exploration, so definitely check out his work. However, it all ultimately boils down to your capacity as a leader to hold that space of humanity: listening, verbalising and showing appreciation, acknowledging learnings, the ability to communicate and build trust. In other words: scoring high on empathy.

Empathy is not about being a pushover; it's about being able to take stock of the data points in your environment and responding appropriately and with care. For example, your team arrives for the first day of a prototyping session or hackathon and you notice that there is a general feel of uncertainty – no one is smiling or joking, some people look nervous, some look bored. Asking them how they're feeling, why they're there and what they would like to see happen centres them, engages them and shows that not only have you noticed their non-verbal cues, but that you care enough to ask and are brave enough to ask the question and hold space for the answer.

No one is expecting miracles. This is messy, unclear, shifting work. The best you can do is start by acknowledging the humans in your organisation and treating them like humans.

PART 3

THE TREASURE IN YOUR OWN BACKYARD

....

Paulo Coelho published *The Alchemist* in 1988 so I don't think this next spoiler is about to ruin anyone's day. The novel follows the story of Santiago, an Andalusian shepherd boy, who consults a Gypsy fortune-teller in search of a meaning for the recurring dream he's been having. Her reply is that it's a prophecy directing him to a treasure in Egypt. Off he goes on a long, winding adventure, and so the story follows, urging the reader to absorb Santiago's lesson of following his dream of finding the treasure.

He travels far and he learns a lot, but when he gets to Egypt... no treasure. Long story short, he goes back home to Spain only to find the treasure was in his 'backyard' all along, buried under the sycamore tree he always used to sleep under when he took his sheep out to graze. The journey was the lesson: the treasure is always at hand, always available.

I'm always reminded of this story about the treasure in the backyard whenever I do design work with organisations or get the opportunity to support and guide them through the new ways of working processes familiar to an innovation culture. I'm reminded of this because the real solution most leaders are looking for to a problem they think they have is often sitting in their own 'backyard': the store front, the back office, the operations teams...

Your own people are where the solution sits – the treasure you've been looking for. They are the ones who deal with your customers; who have to wade through processes and work with the operational knots. They know what your customers need and want, what their pains are. They know the deep systems of your particular context and have the expertise and knowledge bases to your particular area. Your people, sitting in their different units, *are* your customers. But they're got no discretion; they've got no power to prioritise or to influence the conversation around what's happening or what needs to happen. They're very often unaware of strategy or overall organisational needs or gaps. They're very often not asked for their input.

Outsourcing the journey for a cookie-cutter product

Generally speaking, the higher ups don't see their people as a living organism of individuals, but as a complex machine of moving parts to be manipulated and controlled. The larger the machine, the greater the control. And who turns to a working 'machine' and asks it where it's broken or what it needs to be fixed? Instead, unsure of what the problem is or what the solution may be, leaders follow the mechanistic approach, hiring big consultancy groups to do the work on the organisation, to fix it. Often, this process involves asking employees what the answer is, and pitching it as something they came up with as the consultants. Another version is that these big consultancies offer clients a list of pre-designed solutions or enterprise-wide technology platforms that all their competitors are also buying (thereby eroding the competitive advantage of all their clients), with the help of a lot of money, which they then shoehorn into the company with the hopes that some of it fits – and sticks.

It's an all too common occurrence because in South Africa, no-one ever seems to get fired for hiring an expensive global consultancy, regardless of the outcome. Corporate leadership knows something needs to change, feels uncertain about what that is, and is easily soothed by the promise of a straightforward-sounding structure and 1-2-3 steps. But there is a danger in handing over the entire solutioning process of whatever problem you face to an agency that doesn't know your business or your people. Whatever product you get in return is unlikely to be baked in with your organisation's language or its collective wisdom. It's unlikely to speak to your organisation's unique problem.

We're used to seeing this sort of thing happen where an African-based company will appeal to US- or UK-origin consultants who know nothing about the local landscape or culture to solve problems that need a deep and lived experience of this country. We're often directed to learn from and emulate 10- or 15-year-old Silicon Valley tech start-ups, but none of this is very useful for a legacy organisation based in Africa.

A structured problem-solving process is useful, but in over 20 years of working in the organisational effectiveness space, I have yet to come across a cookie-cutter approach that works as a standalone. The problems your company faces will be unique, and the way you solve it is also going to be unique. It's not going to come in the form of an expensive, one-size-fits-all outsourced 'solution', no matter how reassuring that might feel.

You need to strengthen the problem-solving capabilities within the organisation, and you need to build the innovation ecosystem with the people in the ecosystem. That means the process will need to be inclusive, co-created and collaborative.

As a leader within the business or of the business, you need to get down to that sycamore tree in your backyard and find the treasure: the people in your organisation who are going to innovate the organisation.

Your organisation is its own Superman

This is not to say that consultants don't play a role. Apart from the fact that I'm not a turkey that votes for Christmas, it's unrealistic to expect leaders to know everything, to be trained in every process, to be up to date on the latest thought leaders and their work. It's unrealistic to expect people whose days are full with their business to know how to design new systems or be able to devote enough of their time to doing so. It's not always possible to make strategy public by rolling it out across the company or to involve every individual along every step of the way.

But it is possible to bring human-centred problem-solving to collaborative, multi-disciplinary teams. It is possible to involve the skillsets of consultants who will help you to tap into the collective wisdom of your existing employees and maximise their talent, creativity and insights. This is not the old model of creating an exclusive and closed 'innovation hub' in a business. It's about bringing innovative thinking to your entire system so it that infuses human-centred design, agility and radical problem-solving into your existing teams.

Legacy organisations must stop waiting for Superman to fix their problems. A modern organisation is its own Superman. It looks within itself to build itself. It looks internally for what and who it has that it can build on and grow to support and develop a sustainable culture of innovation – a culture of thinking and creating, problem-solving and collaboration. It's built its problem-solving muscles.

Be realistic about your treasure

Looking at the ecosystem that's supporting your innovation processes, even something as 'simple' as infusing new ways of working into your organisation, will kick up some dust.

Innovating the organisation will sometimes feel dangerous. It exposes too many flaws and weaknesses, both in the system and in the people operating the system. It reveals the daunting layers of operational change needed. It reveals how much we don't know about being agile or innovative or new ways of working. And there's no characteristic less associated with the corporate machine than intellectual humility. It might expose how much a certain type of leader might not want to rock the boat or review faulty decisions they may have made.

You need to be realistic, too, about your people. There are some in your team who will be cut out for this work and you'll find them across all levels and areas of your business. These are the people who have the growth mindset to unlearn the stuff that they're good at in their day job. They'll have the intellectual humility to know when they don't know something and the curiosity to learn more. They'll have the grit and flexibility to roll with the complexity and messiness. They'll get that it's all spaghetti. These qualities don't make them better than everyone else, they just make them fit for this particular purpose.

But not everyone will be interested.

A few years back I found myself at lunch with Botswanan-born Hugh Molotsi. He's the founder of messaging platform Ujama and is currently the CEO of the company, but at the time we spoke he was at Intuit as the VC of Innovation. When he started at Intuit they had the vision to be one of the most consistently innovative companies in the world and wanted to get 100% of employees innovating. Twenty years later, Intuit was consistently in the top five innovative companies in the world, but they only had about 15% of people opting into the innovation programme, and that's where it levelled out. I asked him if he considered this a failure. Not at all, he said. Molotsi explained that although they had naively said 100%, the fact was that some people like to be home on time to go to choir practice or go to their sport; they're not motivated by the same things that insatiable problem-solvers might be. Work is a part of their life and they do a great job and they keep the organisation going, but they're not kept up at night wondering how to streamline work efficiencies.

Knowing how to choose your people for working on the ecosystem or the organisation comes down to knowing who your people are. And knowing who your people are and knowing what their capabilities are – and teasing out the best of what they can give – well, that comes down to knowing who you are and whether you're the kind of leader who will inspire that buy-in.

Getting the right people in

To move culture you have to move people. You either have to get rid of assholes or you have to bring in more suitable people. You have to change the balance in the DNA code, splicing it at a people level to create an organisation that is dynamic, collaborative, innovative and prepared for the future. Working on character – how to develop it, build it, strengthen it – is something that has been the ambit of philosophers, anthropologists, psychologists and educators for years now, but it's time to move this into the business realm. To work on the organisation you have to work at the people level. Because no one knows how to work on culture. No one in the world knows how to change a company culture; it's completely hit or miss.

Our obsession with technology and economy as ends in themselves must be shifted. They are merely tools. If we really want to do something different we should become much more fascinated with what makes us human, and tech can help us do that. Tech might change, but very little about being human in the world changes. It's still about relationships and good relationships and ultimately what you do. Did you make a thing? Did you build a thing? Or did you break a thing?

If leadership character traits are the DNA code of culture, then on-boarding or exiting is CRISPR, the technology that's used to find specific bits of corrupt DNA inside a cell and remove or alter them for the improved health of the overall organism. Imagine being able to slice and dice organisational culture at a character level, removing or improving the character traits that underpin the toxic and corrupt elements of the culture. Imagine pipelining leadership candidates with the character traits that will support and build the culture you want for your business – the culture that will best serve modern ways of working with a long-term view for the betterment of the collective.

Of course, existing leaders with the appetite to do so can develop their quality character muscles, and if they choose to do so, become beacons of inspiration for others to do the same. If they're part of the rot and refuse to change, they don't belong in a modern organisation. It should be as simple as that, but of course, it's not. With legacy organisations, it might sometimes feel that a real culture shift is not possible, that it's not down to individual choice because the business is already so infused with the old world that any shift to the new is impossible. Anyone who has spent any time in a closed system like a long-standing company will recognise that elusive quality of a toxic organisational culture; that invisible juggernaut that just drives over any human who might be advocating for the new, which is activated when you try to make any kind of change. Even if the people around that table have asked for it, even if they're not playing the role of Grendel's Mom, it's as if the humans aren't running the organisation anymore, like there's a ghost in the machine of old cultural mores. I've seen really good people find their place at the head of the table and then suddenly appear to be channelling Voldemort.

How do you embed a new culture, one that builds and grows a strong, self-supporting innovation ecosystem? The only way to change culture is to change the people creating that culture. If culture is the sum of all the character traits held by the most influential people in the business, the only way to change that culture is to on-board more of those people with good character strengths, or design an exit strategy for those less desirable traits. But how do you get rid of a high-level Voldemort? That I don't know. Maybe it's a consequence of tipping the scales. If each person started doing the individual work could there ultimately be a tipping point when there are so many people of good character inside an organisation that the machine's no longer running it?

How do we measure character?

Measuring character really is where the next big problem lies for me. So let's say we starting hiring (and firing) for character. Who judges good character? When you're putting your team together for a new process it's easy enough to see who has the grit and growth mindset to really take on the challenge since they're jumping through the hoops to get involved. But what about creating a measurable framework to formalise and scale?

We've seen this sort of quantifying attempt happen with personality tests. Apart from the fact that personality is not what we're after, we also know now that there is bias when people self-assess. For example: "X is my boss, she wants me to complete this innovation profiler. I've heard her say that what we really need in the company are less big talkers and more doers, so every question I answer I say I have a bias for execution, I like getting things done, I'm very good at getting things done, if you need something done I'm your guy." So however you choose to present yourself is only going to reveal a superficial assessment of outward-facing razzmatazz.

In Kiel's study, the CEOs who thought that they were of good character rated themselves highly, while their staff on the other hand rated them poorly. The reverse was also true. The CEOs who presented themselves with some humility were shown to be superstars by their people. Interestingly, the same level of honesty doesn't exist in peer reviews. 360-degree reviews are all time-consuming bullshit that almost never work. People are too keen to paint their colleagues in a good light for their own best interests. You know people are having coffees with each other and striking Pollyanna deals over the table: you say this nice thing about me and I'll say this nice thing about you. And traditional reference checks during recruitment? Barely useful.

The only way to get a real picture on someone is through reliable, impersonal data. But how to go about collecting that?

Painting a picture of character

There's very early-stage clumsy character-based scoring that's starting to emerge. In his book *The Originals*, Adam Grant refers to a study that looked into the call-centre industry, which was really suffering globally from massive attrition rates, to find out why this was happening. Typically, the approach would be to trawl the HR data to assess where the weak links are, but instead, the researcher asked for IT data and found two types of people: those agents who had simply kept the default browser on the desktop and those who had replaced the default browser with Chrome. They then cross-referenced these data points with HR data and found an interesting correlation. Those who had replaced the default browser with their own choice were three times more productive, interesting, promotable, better at sales and so on – basically better and much happier employees.

Sure, one could argue that as security risks increase, your choice of browser is increasingly limited by what is stipulated by the IT department, but there are other data points we could use to score character. A lot of the information is probably already available in your CV and background checks, it's just about how the information is processed. The question is what other information can we start reconciling? Kinds of apps downloaded, social media profile, courses you've completed and under what circumstances, background relative to where you find yourself today... we need to know what you do, not what you say you do. If you've run 20 Comrades marathons, written a book, started a side hustle or clawed your way up from poverty, you've probably got grit. Maybe people who have downloaded certain kinds of apps tend to have a higher curiosity score than people who haven't. Maybe those who've undergone self-awareness programmes or better relating courses might score higher on other-centredness. Maybe, instead of peer reviews and reference letters, there is a framework in place to get character feedback from past clients and colleagues.

There is some precedent for this already in credit checks, and specifically how some micro-lending platforms rate lenders. For example, on the Jumo platform, if you click 'yes' on a text asking you if you need a micro loan and accept the T&Cs, an algorithm scours your online profiles and connections to gauge your reliability as a first-time borrower. Based on data, you're then presented with an offer which prices the credit. It might take 20 years to get to some point of measuring leadership character strengths accurately, but this is a start.

CONCLUSION

Up until now, the great innovations of our time have been driven by profitability rather than human need and an awareness of our limited resources. The underlying culture of legacy organisations has been one of gouging, value extraction and short-term benefit. We find ourselves trapped in vast global economic systems that are corrupt and drive systemic inequality. We're burning through our resources at a rate that can no longer be mitigated by our excuses to drive 'economic growth'.

It's clear that the status quo is no longer serving us. We can't pretend that we don't have to change. We can't hide behind the excuse of ignorance enjoyed by our ancestors. We have hard data now confirming that human action has been the main driver of global environmental change since the Industrial Revolution. We're aware of the cost of our actions. We are conscious and with this consciousness comes responsibility.

To action this responsibility, we can't be doing more of the same. As Albert Einstein said: "We cannot solve our problems with the same thinking we used when we created them."

Whether we want to or not, there is no going back to business as usual. Setting up an innovation hub to brainstorm new products for your company is no longer enough to weather the upheavals we are facing, whether they be economic, social or environmental.

To move into a future space, we must consider human needs, human relationships and the ethical response of stewardship to the environment. There is no other way to go about it if we want to build a sustainable future for ourselves and those who come after us. Because right now, we're not super worthy ancestors for our kids and subsequent generations. We've part of a huge fucking mess and there's a lot of work to do to un-mess ourselves. There's a staggering waste of human potential in these corporate contexts, where people are not doing work they're passionate about and leave their brain at the door when they arrive. We can't afford to waste this potential anymore. This is a moment of opportunity for a Great Correction. I believe that the bulk of this work, and the reach it can have, sits within the ambit of legacy organisations to affect. But to do this, we'll need to disrupt the very culture that has brought us here. We have to innovate the system. To do so, we must think of innovation differently; it must become an organisational imperative, a way of working that seeps into the culture, and for this to happen we need to look to the custodians of that culture, the leaders and leadership teams, and ask: Are they people of good character who can lead us into a better future? Are you? Am I?

It's complex, messy, ambiguous work. It's that bowl of spaghetti Kahn was talking about. And this theory that leadership character is the unlock to sustainable and effective corporate innovation? Well, I believe it's one big, juicy mouthful.

REFERENCES

3D Eye. (2015). *The Educators, KIPP Schools and Multi-intelligent Approaches to Education*. Available from: https://3diassociates.wordpress.com/2015/11/25/the-educators-kipp-schools-and-multi-intelligent-approaches-to-education/

Ackoff, L.R., & Rovin, S. (2003). *Redesigning Society*. Redwood City, CA: Stanford University Press.

Alldredge, K., & Grimmelt, A. (2021). *Understanding the ever-evolving, always-surprising consumer*. Available from: https://www.mckinsey.com/industries/consumer-packaged-goods/our-insights/understanding-the-ever-evolving-always-surprising-consumer

Ambridge, B. (2016). *Open wide: why yawning reveals much about your level of empathy*. Available from: https://www.theguardian.com/lifeandstyle/2016/mar/27/what-does-yawning-say-about-you-quiz

Anderson, N., Potočnik, K., & Zhou, J. (2014). Innovation and Creativity in Organizations: A State-of-the-Science Review, Prospective Commentary, and Guiding Framework. *Journal of Management, 40*(5): 1297-1333. Available from: https://journals.sagepub.com/doi/abs/10.1177/0149206314527128

Arthur, R. (2018). *Bad Chicago Cops Spread Their Misconduct Like a Disease*. Available from: https://theintercept.com/2018/08/16/chicago-police-misconduct-social-network/

Aziz, A. (2020). *Global Study Reveals Consumers Are Four To Six Times More Likely To Purchase, Protect And Champion Purpose-Driven Companies*. Available from: https://www.forbes.com/sites/afdhelaziz/2020/06/17/global-study-reveals-consumers-are-four-to-six-times-more-likely-to-purchase-protect-and-champion-purpose-driven-companies/?sh=712a7093435f

Barrett, J.L. (2017). Intellectual humility. *The Journal of Positive Psychology, 12*(1): 1-2.

Baumgartner, J. (2010). *The Critical Role of Trust in the Innovation Process*. Available from: https://innovationmanagement.se/imtool-articles/the-critical-role-of-trust-in-the-innovation-process/

Baumgartner, J.P. (n.d.). *Articles by Jeffrey Paul Baumgartner*. Available from: https://muckrack.com/jeffrey-paul-baumgartner/articles

BBC. (2014). *John Walker's Friction Light*. Available from: http://www.bbc.co.uk/ahistoryoftheworld/objects/hQR9oN5LTeCLcuKfPDMJ9A

Beheshti, N. (2018). *Is It Truly Lonely at the Top?* Available from: https://www.forbes.com/sites/nazbeheshti/2018/09/26/is-it-lonely-at-the-top/?sh=767e963869c5

Berger, W. (2015). *Why Curious People are Destined for the C-Suite*. Available from: https://hbr.org/2015/09/why-curious-people-are-destined-for-the-c-suite

Big Think. (2018). *Why giving gifts brings you more happiness than receiving them.* Available from: https://bigthink.com/personal-growth/why-its-better-to-give-gifts-than-to-receive-according-to-science?rebelltitem=2#rebelltitem2

Bolden-Barrett, V. (2017). *Study: Disengaged employees can cost companies up to $550B a year.* Available from: https://www.hrdive.com/news/study-disengaged-employees-can-cost-companies-up-to-550b-a-year/437606/

Borody, B. (2020). *Being empathetic is important. Can you learn empathy?* Available from: https://takealtus.com/2020/07/empathy-2/

Brooks. A. (2022). *Why It's So Lonely at the Top.* Available from: https://arthurbrooks.com/article/why-its-so-lonely-at-the-top/

Brower, T. (2019). *Want More Innovative Solutions? Start With Empathy.* Available from: https://www.forbes.com/sites/tracybrower/2019/01/20/want-more-innovative-solutions-start-with-empathy/?sh=5fca64962211

Brown, S., Gray, D., HcHardy, J., & Taylor, K. (2015). Employee trust and workplace performance. *Elsevier Journal of Economic Behavior & Organization, 116*: 361-378. Available from: https://www.sciencedirect.com/science/article/pii/S0167268115001365

Burns, T., Ellsworth, D., Field, E., & Harris, T. (2021). *The diversity imperative in retail.* Available from: https://www.mckinsey.com/industries/retail/our-insights/the-diversity-imperative-in-retail

Callagher, L., & Smith, P. (2017). Innovation awards: Reward, Recognition, and Ritual. *International Journal of Innovation Management, 21*(1): 1740006. Available from: https://www.researchgate.net/publication/317152476_INNOVATION_AWARDS_REWARD_RECOGNITION_AND_RITUAL

Casper. (n.d.). *TakeCasper is now TakeAltus!* Available from: https://takecasper.com/2020/07/empathy-2/

Castelli, P.A., & Wan Abdul Rahman, A. (2013). *The impact of empathy on leadership effectiveness among business leaders in the United States and Malaysia.* Available from: https://www.researchgate.net/publication/283721655_The_impact_of_empathy_on_leadership_effectiveness_among_business_leaders_in_the_United_States_and_Malaysia

Center for Creative Leadership. (2020). *The Importance of Empathy in the Workplace.* Available from: https://www.ccl.org/articles/leading-effectively-articles/empathy-in-the-workplace-a-tool-for-effective-leadership/

Chamorro-Premuzic, T. (2017). *What Happens When Leaders Lack Curiosity?* Available from: https://www.forbes.com/sites/tomaspremuzic/2017/03/06/what-happens-when-leaders-lack-curiosity/?sh=2a91f5776b74

Clarke, J., & Goldman, R. (2021). *Cognitive vs. Emotional Empathy.* Available from: https://www.verywellmind.com/cognitive-and-emotional-empathy-4582389

Cooper, B.K., Sarros, J.C., & Santora, J.C. *The Character of Leadership.* Available from: https://iveybusinessjournal.com/publication/the-character-of-leadership/

Cordy, E. (2018). *Why Curiosity is the Key to Workplace Innovation*. Available from: https://www.leaderonomics.com/articles/business/curiosity-workplace-innovation

Currin, G. (2020). *Why are humans so curious?* Available from: https://www.livescience.com/why-are-humans-curious.html

Darwin, C. (n.d.). *The Descent of Man*. Available from: https://charles-darwin.classic-literature.co.uk/the-descent-of-man/ebook-page-72.asp

Darwin, C. (n.d.). *The Victorian Web*. Available from: http://www.victorianweb.org/science/darwin/sympathy.html

Daskal, L. (2018). *How to be an Empathetic Leader*. Available from: https://www.lollydaskal.com/leadership/how-to-be-an-empathetic-leader/

Daskal, L. (2019). *The Best Survival Guide for a Toxic Workplace*. Available from: https://www.lollydaskal.com/leadership/the-best-survival-guide-for-a-toxic-workplace/

Daskal, L. (2020). *How to Build Trust in a Room When You Need It Most*. Available from: https://www.lollydaskal.com/leadership/how-to-build-trust-in-a-room-when-you-need-it-most/

Davis, N., & Mulcahy, S. (2018). *The power of trust and values in the Fourth Industrial Revolution*. Available from: https://www.weforum.org/agenda/2018/10/power-trust-and-values-fourth-industrial-revolution/

De Braine, R.T., & Verrier, D. (2007). Leadership, character and its development: A qualitative exploration. *SA Journal of Human Resource Management, 5*(1): 1-10. Available from: https://www.researchgate.net/publication/47727845_Leadership_character_and_its_development_A_qualitative_exploration

Desai, R. (2020). *We've Completely Misunderstood 'Survival of the Fittest,' Evolutionary Biologists Say*. Available from: https://theswaddle.com/weve-completely-misunderstood-survival-of-the-fittest-evolutionary-biologists-say/

Dovey, K. (2009). The Role of Trust in Innovation. *The Learning Organization 16*(4): 311-325.

Dweck, C. (2014). Developing a Growth Mindset with Carol Dweck. Available from: https://www.youtube.com/watch?v=hiiEeMN7vbQ

EdUpStairs NPC. (2019). *Dr Carol Dweck's Research into Growth Mindset Changed Education Forever*. Available from: https://edupstairs.org/growth-mindset/

Ensemble Consulting Group. (2022). *A hierarchy required by nature.* Available from: https://ensembleconsultinggroup.com/a-hierarchy-required-by-nature/

Entis, L. (2014). *Why Peter Thiel's Philosophy on Hiring Is Hurting Silicon Valley*. Available from: https://www.entrepreneur.com/article/237677

Eva, N., Robin, M., Sendjaya, S., van Dierendonck, D., & Liden, R.C. (2019). Servant Leadership: A systematic review and call for future research. *The Leadership Quarterly, 30*(1): 111-132. Available from: https://www.sciencedirect.com/science/article/pii/S1048984317307774?via%3Dihub

Forbes. (2012). *Enron 10 Years After – From Bad to Worse*. Available from: https://www.forbes.com/sites/thestreet/2012/04/23/enron-10-years-after-from-bad-to-worse/?sh=7ec6574f2c65

Francis, T., & Hoefel, F. (2018). *'True Gen': Generation Z and its implications for companies*. Available from: https://www.mckinsey.com/industries/consumer-packaged-goods/our-insights/true-gen-generation-z-and-its-implications-for-companies

Gashparac, B. (2020). *This Shopping Trolley Theory Will Determine Whether Or Not You're A Good Person*. Available from: https://www.wsfm.com.au/lifestyle/this-shopping-trolley-theory-will-determine-whether-or-not-youre-a-good-person/

Glover, P. (2021). *Three Successful Ways to Practice Empathetic Leadership in the Workplace*. Available from: https://www.forbes.com/sites/forbescoachescouncil/2021/06/15/three-successful-ways-to-practice-empathetic-leadership-in-the-workplace/?sh=44b14d6816cc

Gourguechon, P. (2017). *Empathy Is an Essential Leadership Skill – And There's Nothing Soft About It*. Available from: https://www.forbes.com/sites/prudygourguechon/2017/12/26/empathy-is-an-essential-leadership-skill-and-theres-nothing-soft-about-it/?sh=75c115bd2b9d

Graham-Leviss, K. (2016). *The 5 Skills That Innovative Leaders have in Common*. Available from: https://hbr.org/2016/12/the-5-skills-that-innovative-leaders-have-in-common

Grahek, M.S., Thompson, A.D., & Toliver, A. (2010). The Character to Lead: A Closer Look at Character in Leadership. *American Psychological Association, 62*(4): 270-290. Available from: https://worthyleadership.com/wp-content/uploads/2014/01/the-character-to-lead.pdf

Grant, A. (2014). *Give and Take: Why Helping Others Drives Our Success*. New York: Penguin Books.

Gray, A. (2016). *The 10 skills you need to thrive in the Fourth Industrial Revolution*. Available from: https://www.weforum.org/agenda/2016/01/the-10-skills-you-need-to-thrive-in-the-fourth-industrial-revolution/

Greater Good Science Center. (n.d.). *What is Altruism?* Available from: https://greatergood.berkeley.edu/topic/altruism/definition#:~:text=Evolutionary%20scientists%20speculate%20that%20altruism,the%20survival%20of%20our%20species.&text=This%20does%20not%20mean%20that,to%20act%20in%20either%20direction

Green, M.T., Rodriquez, R.A., Wheeler, C.A., & Baggerly-Hinojosa, B. (2015). *Servant Leadership: A Quantitative Review of Instruments and Related Findings*. Available from: https://csuepress.columbusstate.edu/cgi/viewcontent.cgi?article=1022&context=sltp

Greenleaf, R. (2020). *What is Servant Leadership?* Available from: https://www.greenleaf.org/what-is-servant-leadership/

Hartikainen, J. (2019). *Organization as living organism and complex adaptive system*. Available from: https://www.tietoevry.com/en/blog/2019/10/organization-as-living-organism-and-complex-adaptive-system/

Harvard Business Review. (2015a). Leadership Measuring the Return on Character. *Harvard Business Review, 96*(4): 20-21.

Harvard Business Review. (2015b). *The Business Case for Purpose*. Available from: https://assets.ey.com/content/dam/ey-sites/ey-com/en_gl/topics/digital/ey-the-business-case-for-purpose.pdf

Havard Business Review. (2019). *How Leaders Build Trust*. Available from: https://hbr.org/tip/2019/06/how-leaders-build-trust

Hearn, S. (2018). *8 Reasons 360-Degree Feedback Fails*. Available from: https://www.clearreview.com/360-degree-feedback-fails/

Heathfield, S.M. (2019). *The Power of Positive Employee Recognition*. Available from: https://www.thebalancecareers.com/the-power-of-positive-employee-recognition-1919054

Hemmelder, V., & Blanchard, T. (2917). *Why Humans Are Hard-Wired for Curiosity*. Available from: https://www.huffpost.com/entry/why-humans-are-hardwired-_b_11984748

Hinojosa, P. (n.d.). *Why and how servant leadership is good for business*. Available from: https://www.insperity.com/blog/servant-leadership/

History of Information. (1961). *Arthur C. Clarke Publishes "Dial F for Frankenstein," an Inspiration for Tim Berners-Lee*. Available from: https://historyofinformation.com/detail.php?id=2137

Howes, A. (2016). *Is Innovation in Human Nature?* Available from: https://medium.com/@antonhowes/is-innovation-in-human-nature-48c2578e27ba

Idea to Value. (n.d.). *Curiosity: The Key to Creativity and Innovation*. Available from: https://www.ideatovalue.com/crea/khkim/2017/06/curiosity-key-creativity-innovation/

Ines, E. (2018). *Lonely at the top? Do me a favour!* Available from: https://www.london.edu/think/lonely-at-the-top-do-me-a-favour

Inesi, M.E., Gruenfeld, D.H., & Galinsky, A.D. (2012). How power corrupts relationships: Cynical attributions for others' generous acts. *Elsevier Journal of Experimental Social Psychology, 48*(4): 795-803. Available from: https://www.sciencedirect.com/science/article/abs/pii/S002210311200011X

Jajal, T.D. (2018). *The Helper's High: The Neurobiology of Helping Others*. Available from: https://tjajal.medium.com/the-helpers-high-the-neurobiology-of-helping-others-ea155e22bd3c

Johnson, K.H. (2018). *The Most Important Skill For 21st-Century Success*. Available from: https://www.forbes.com/sites/kevinhjohnson/2018/07/31/the-most-important-skill-for-21st-century-success/?sh=4b8e25f532c8

Kamensky, J. (2018). *The Role of Curiosity in Innovation*. Available from: http://www.businessofgovernment.org/blog/role-curiosity-innovation

Katz, D. (2017). *Is It Really Lonely at The Top?* Available from: https://executivevine.com/executive/articles/is-it-really-lonely-at-the-top/

Kellogg Insight. (2009). *Losing Touch: Power diminishes perception and perspective*. Available from: https://insight.kellogg.northwestern.edu/article/losing-touch

Kellogg Insight. (2016). *Is It Really Lonely at the Top?* Available from: https://insight.kellogg.northwestern.edu/article/is-it-really-lonely-at-the-top

Kelly, N. (2021). *How to Train and Practice Empathy with Other Leaders*. Available from: https://www.entrepreneur.com/article/377546

Kidd, C., & Hayden, B.Y. (2015). The psychology and neuroscience of curiosity. *Neuron, 88*(3): 449-460. Available from: https://www.ncbi.nlm.nih.gov/pmc/articles/PMC4635443/

Kiel, F. (2013). *Psychopaths in the C-suite.* Available from: https://www.youtube.com/watch?v=vqBPZR63vfA

Kleiner, A. (2010). *The Organization is Alive.* Available from: https://www.strategy-business.com/article/00028?gko=6f9cb

Konrath, S., O'Brien, E.H., & Hsing, C. (2011). Changes in Dispositional Empathy in American College Students Over Time: A Meta-Analysis. *Personality and Social Psychology Review, 15*(2): 180-98.

Leadership Digest. (2020). *The Power of Gratitude.* Available from: https://innovation-thinking.com/2020/11/11/the-power-of-gratitude/

Leadership IQ. (n.d.). *Research: How to Build Trust in the Workplace.* Available from: https://www.leadershipiq.com/blogs/leadershipiq/research-how-to-build-trust-in-the-workplace

Leadership Worth Following (LLC). (2018). *Still Relevant, Worthy Leadership Model Marks 10 Years.* Available from: https://worthyleadership.com/still-relevant-worthy-leadership-model-marks-10-years/

Leary, M.R. (2018). *The Psychology of Intellectual Humility.* Available from: https://www.templeton.org/wp-content/uploads/2020/08/JTF_Intellectual_Humility_final.pdf

Leavitt, P. (2002). *Rewarding Innovation.* Available from: http://www.providersedge.com/docs/km_articles/rewarding_innovation.pdf

Lehman, A. (2009). *Neoteny, Acceleration and Evolution.* Available from: http://www.neoteny.org/2009/12/14/neoteny-acceleration-and-evolution/

Lekutis, C. (2013). *Cell phone inventor to address the tower workers who installed the backbone for the "Brick".* Available from: http://wirelessestimator.com/content/articles/?pagename=Martin%20%22Marty%22%20Cooper%20-%20Inventor%20of%20the%20cell%20phone

London Business School. (n.d.). *Ena Inesi: Associate Professor of Organisational Behaviour.* Available from: https://www.london.edu/faculty-and-research/faculty-profiles/i/inesi-me

MacMillan, A. (2017). *Being Generous Really Does Make You Happier.* Available from: https://time.com/4857777/generosity-happiness-brain/

Mineo, L. (2017). *Good genes are nice, but joy is better.* Available from: https://news.harvard.edu/gazette/story/2017/04/over-nearly-80-years-harvard-study-has-been-showing-how-to-live-a-healthy-and-happy-life/

Molokhia, D. (2018). *The Importance of Being Curious.* Available from: https://www.harvardbusiness.org/the-importance-of-being-curious/

Mourkogiannis, N. (2006). *Purpose: The Starting Point of Great Companies.* New York: Palgrave Macmillan.

Munn, M.W. (1998). *Beyond Business as Usual: Practical Lessons in Accessing New Dimensions.* New York: Butterworth-Heinemann, p.57.

Murphy, M. (2018). *Research Shows the Quickest Way to Build Trust with Your Employees*. Available from: https://www.forbes.com/sites/markmurphy/2018/06/17/research-shows-the-quickest-way-to-build-trust-with-your-employees/?sh=366375f96757

Nagji, B., & Tuff, G. (2012). *Managing Your Innovation Portfolio*. Available from: https://hbr.org/2012/05/managing-your-innovation-portfolio

National Institutes of Health (NIH). (2007). *Brain Imaging Reveals Joys of Giving*. Available from: https://www.nih.gov/news-events/nih-research-matters/brain-imaging-reveals-joys-giving

Navarrete, J. (2017). *Master Thesis on millennial psychology and employee motivation*. Available from: https://www.researchgate.net/project/Master-Thesis-on-millennial-psychology-and-employee-motivation

Nelson, R. (2010). *Pixar's Randy Nelson on the Collaborative Age*. Available from: https://www.youtube.com/watch?v=QhXJe8ANws8

New York Times. (2016). *This Great-Grandmother Coaches an Olympic Champion. Now Let Her By*. Available from: https://www.nytimes.com/2016/08/16/sports/olympics/wayde-van-niekerk-coach-anna-sofia-botha.html

Nicholson, J. (2017). *What Caused Enron to Collapse?* Available from: https://bizfluent.com/how-does-4911332-what-caused-enron-collapse.html

O'Brien, D., Main, A., & Kounkel, S. (2019). *Purpose is everything: How brands that authentically lead with purpose are changing the nature of business today*. Available from: https://www2.deloitte.com/us/en/insights/topics/marketing-and-sales-operations/global-marketing-trends/2020/purpose-driven-companies.html/%23endnote-sup-7.html

O'Brien, J.M. (2007). *Meet the PayPal mafia*. Available from: https://money.cnn.com/2007/11/13/magazines/fortune/paypal_mafia.fortune/index.htm

O'Grady, M. (2019). *2 Ways to Practice Gratitude with Your Children*. Available from: https://www.viacharacter.org/topics/articles/two-ways-to-practice-gratitude-with-children

Peregrine Global Services. (2020). *Enron – The Smartest Guy in the Room*. Available from: https://vimeo.com/424073216

Pink, D.H. (2009). *Drive: The surprising Truth about What Motivates Us*. New York, NY: Riverhead Books

Porter, T. (n.d.). *Intellectual Humility: Recognizing the limitations of your knowledge*. Available from: https://characterlab.org/playbooks/intellectual-humility/

PWC White Paper. (2015). *Understanding the value and drivers of organizational trust: Trust insight*. Available from: https://www.pwc.com/my/en/assets/trust/trust-insight-understanding-the-value-and-drivers-of-organisational-trust.pdf

PWC. (2016). *Redefining business success in a changing world: CEO Survey*. Available from: https://www.pwc.com/gx/en/ceo-survey/2016/landing-page/pwc-19th-annual-global-ceo-survey.pdf

PWC. (2019). *20 years inside the mind of the CEO...What's next?* Available from: https://www.chieflearningofficer.com/wp-content/uploads/sites/3/2019/08/pwc-ceo-survey-report-2017.pdf

Rao, S.S. (2011). *Moving From a 'Me' to an 'Other-Centered' Universe*. Available from: https://www.huffpost.com/entry/how-to-be-happy-moving-fr_b_570730

Resnick, B. (2019). *Intellectual humility: the importance of knowing you might be wrong*. Available from: https://www.vox.com/science-and-health/2019/1/4/17989224/intellectual-humility-explained-psychology-replication

Riche, R. (n.d.). *One Clear Message: 5 elements for building trust in the workplace*. Available from: https://www.oneclearmessage.co.za/5-elements-for-building-trust-in-the-workplace/

Ries, E. (2022). *A Letter to our Future*. Available from: https://blog.ltse.com/the-long-term-stock-exchange-opens-for-business-38b13f51e87b

Riess, H. (2017). The Science of Empathy. *Journal of Patient Experience, 4*(2): 74-77. Available from: https://www.ncbi.nlm.nih.gov/pmc/articles/PMC5513638/

Robbins, M. (2019). *Why Employees Need Both Recognition and Appreciation*. Available from: https://hbr.org/2019/11/why-employees-need-both-recognition-and-appreciation

Rokach, A. (2014). Leadership and Loneliness. *International Journal of Leadership and Change, 2*(1): 6. Available from: https://digitalcommons.wku.edu/cgi/viewcontent.cgi?article=1014&context=ijlc

Root-Bernstein, R., Allen, L., Beach, L., & Bhadula, R. (2008). Arts Foster Scientific Success: Avocations of Nobel, National Academy, Royal Society, and Sigma Xi Members. *Journal of Psychology of Science and Technology, 1*(2): 51-63.

Ross, J. (2013). *How Other-Centered Are You?* Available from: https://jeffrossblog.com/2013/12/23/how-other-centered-are-you/

Rowland, D. (n.d.). *Dotoku - Education in Morality*. Available from: https://www.international-excellence.com/blog-1/73-uncategorised/389-dotoku-education-in-morality

Ruiz, C. (2019). *The Importance of Curiosity in Leadership*. Available from: https://innerwill.org/the-importance-of-curiosity-in-leadership/

Sahi, R. (2018). *What is empathy?* Available from: https://www.psychologyinaction.org/psychology-in-action-1/2018/2/21/what-is-empathy

Saxena, A. (2016). *High-Trust Matters*. Available from: https://www.greatplacetowork.com/resources/blog/high-trust-matters

Schwartz, T., & Porath, C. (2014). *The Power of Meeting Your Employees' Needs*. Available from: https://hbr.org/2014/06/the-power-of-meeting-your-employees-needs

Science Daily. (2018a). *Genes play a role in empathy*. Available from: https://www.sciencedaily.com/releases/2018/03/180312085124.htm

Science Daily. (2018b). *The joy of giving lasts longer than the joy of getting*. Available from: https://www.sciencedaily.com/releases/2018/12/181220080008.htm

ScienceDaily. (2020). *New insights into the mechanisms of neuroplasticity*. Available from: https://www.sciencedaily.com/releases/2020/12/201204110206.htm

Servaes, H., & Tamayo, A. (2017). *The Role of Social Capital in Corporations: A Review*. Available from: https://papers.ssrn.com/sol3/papers.cfm?abstract_id=2933393

Shalett, L. (2020). *Why Corporate Directors Need to Focus on Trust.* Available from: https://www.shrm.org/executive/resources/people-strategy-journal/summer2020/Pages/feature-shalett.aspx

Siddique, H. (2016). *Ans Botha: 74-year-old who coached Wayde van Niekerk to 400m gold.* Available from: https://www.theguardian.com/sport/2016/aug/16/ans-botha-74-coach-wayde-van-niekerk-400m-world-record-rio-olympics

Somerville, K. (n.d.). *The Hidden Power of Intellectual Humility.* Available from: https://thedecisionlab.com/insights/society/the-hidden-power-of-intellectual-humility/

Stafford, T. (2012). *Why are we so curious?* Available from: https://www.bbc.com/future/article/20120618-why-are-we-so-curious

Stanford Encyclopedia of Philosophy. (2019). *Empathy.* Available from: https://plato.stanford.edu/entries/empathy/#HisInt

Stobierski, T. (2018). *How to Become a More Empathetic Leader.* Available from: https://www.northeastern.edu/graduate/blog/become-an-empathetic-leader/

Stockton-on-Tees Borough Council. (n.d.). *John Walker - Inventor of the Friction Match.* Available from: https://heritage.stockton.gov.uk/articles/people/john-walker-inventor-of-the-friction-match/

Strauss, M. (2012). *Ten Inventions Inspired by Science Fiction.* Available from: https://www.smithsonianmag.com/science-nature/ten-inventions-inspired-by-science-fiction-128080674/?page=10

Success Factory. (n.d.). *15 Ideas for Rewarding Innovation in the Workplace.* Available from: https://www.thesuccessfactory.co.uk/blog/11-ideas-for-rewarding-innovation-in-the-workplace

Systematic Incentive Thinking. (2018). *How Companies Incentivize Innovation.* Available from: https://www.sitsite.com/wp-content/uploads/2018/09/How-Companies-Incentivize-Innovation-E-version-May-2013.pdf

Tanveer Naseer Leadership. (2011). *Empathy in Leadership – 10 Reasons Why It Matters.* Available from: https://www.tanveernaseer.com/why-empathy-matters-in-leadership/

Tanveer Naseer Leadership. (n.d.). *A Timely Reminder of The Power Of Empathy In Leadership.* Available from: https://www.tanveernaseer.com/the-growing-importance-of-empathy-in-leadership-today/

Tes Magazine. (2019). *Pedagogy Focus: Growth mindset.* Available from: https://www.tes.com/news/pedagogy-focus-growth-mindset

The Bassett Firm. (2017). *In Defense of Others-Centeredness.* Available from: https://www.thebassettfirm.com/blog/2017/08/in-defense-of-others-centeredness/

The HR Lounge. (n.d.). *What motivates employees: carrots or sticks?* Available from: http://www.thehrlounge.co.uk/what-motivates-employees-carrots-or-sticks

Tibbitts, K. (2014). *Rate-of-learning: the most valuable startup compensation.* Available from: https://kyletibbitts.com/rate-of-learning-the-most-valuable-startup-compensation-56dddc17fa42

Trapp, R. (2013). *It Really Is Lonely At The Top.* Available from: https://www.forbes.com/sites/rogertrapp/2013/10/09/lonely-at-the-top/?sh=321e5c6f5fd2

Turchin, P. (2013). *Selfish Genes Made Me Do It! (Part I).* Available from: https://thisviewoflife.com/blog/selfish-genes-made-me-do-it-part-i

University of Connecticut. (n.d.). *What is Intellectual Humility?* Available from: https://humilityandconviction.uconn.edu/blank/what-is-intellectual-humility/

University of Michigan. (2010). *Empathy: College students don't have as much as they used to.* Available from: https://news.umich.edu/empathy-college-students-don-t-have-as-much-as-they-used-to/

Unsriana, L., & Ningrum, R. (2018). The Character Formation of Children in Japan: A Study of Japanese Children Textbook on Moral Education (Doutoku). *Lingua Cultura, 12*(4): 363.

van Berlo, E., Díaz-Loyo, A.P., Juárez-Mora, O.E., Kret, M.E., & Massen, J.J.M. (2020). Experimental evidence for yawn contagion in orangutans (*Pongo pygmaeus*). *Scientific Reports, 10*(22251). Available from: https://www.nature.com/articles/s41598-020-79160-x

Warden, T. (n.d.). *The role of Rewards in Creating a Culture of Innovation.* Available from: https://focus.kornferry.com/reward-and-benefits/the-role-of-rewards-in-creating-a-culture-of-innovation/

Wasserman, N. (2013). *Founder's Dilemmas: Relationships.* Available from: https://www.youtube.com/watch?v=elWpveNLNLc

Western Governors University (WGU). (2019). *What is a growth mindset? 8 steps to develop one.* Available from: https://www.wgu.edu/blog/what-is-growth-mindset-8-steps-develop-one1904.html

Whitaker, R. (2008). *Arthur C Clarke: science fiction turns to fact.* Available from: https://www.independent.co.uk/news/science/arthur-c-clarke-science-fiction-turns-to-fact-799519.html

Wikipedia. (2022a). *Servant leadership.* Available from: https://en.wikipedia.org/wiki/Servant_leadership

Wikipedia. (2022b). *Tim Berners-Lee.* Available from: https://en.wikipedia.org/wiki/Tim_Berners-Lee

Williams, D.K. (2017). *Never Fear: 3 Ways to Stay Innovative Without Fear.* Available from: https://medium.com/the-mission/never-fear-3-ways-to-stay-innovative-without-fear-8b0148dc5857

Woo, S.E., Chernyshenko, O.S., Longley, A., Zhang, Zhi-Xue, Chiu, Chi-Yue., & Stark, S.E. (2014). Openness to Experience: Its Lower Level Structure, Measurement, and Cross-Cultural Equivalence. *Journal of Personality Assessment, 96*(1): 29-45. Available from: https://www.tandfonline.com/doi/abs/10.1080/00223891.2013.806328

World Athletics. (2017). *Botha's recipe for coaching success: patience, endurance and perseverance.* Available from: https://www.worldathletics.org/news/feature/anna-botha-iaaf-coaching-achievement-award

World Economic Forum. (2019). *The Global Risks Report 2019 14th Edition.* Available from: https://www3.weforum.org/docs/WEF_Global_Risks_Report_2019.pdf

Wright, R. (2001). *The Man Who Invented the Web*. Available from: http://content.time.com/time/magazine/article/0,9171,137689,00.html

Your Dictionary. (n.d.). *Tim Berners-Lee Biography*. Available from: https://biography.yourdictionary.com/tim-berners-lee

YouTube. (2016). *Rio Reply: Men's 400m Sprint Final*. Available from: https://www.youtube.com/watch?v=xG91krXuxyw

Zak, P.J. (2017). *The Neuroscience of Trust*. Available from: https://hbr.org/2017/01/the-neuroscience-of-trust

Zenger, J., & Folkman, J. (2019). *The 3 Elements of Trust*. Available from: https://hbr.org/2019/02/the-3-elements-of-trust

Zeno Group. (2020). *2020 Zeno Strength of Purpose Study*. Available from: https://www.zenogroup.com/insights/2020-zeno-strength-purpose

Zmigrod, L., Zmigrod, S., Rentfrow, P.J., & Robbins, T.W. (2019). The psychological roots of intellectual humility: The role of intelligence and cognitive flexibility. *Elsevier, 141*: 200-208. Available from: https://www.sciencedirect.com/science/article/pii/S0191886919300285

INDEX